HOWARD UNIVERSITY
in the
WORLD WARS

HOWARD
UNIVERSITY
·············· *in the* ··············
WORLD WARS

MEN AND WOMEN SERVING THE NATION

Lopez D. Matthews Jr., PhD

THE
History
PRESS

Published by The History Press
Charleston, SC
www.historypress.com

First published 2018

ISBN 9781540235633

Library of Congress Control Number: 2018940071

CONTENTS

THE IMPORTANCE OF MILITARY
SERVICE AND THE HOWARD LEGACY

Military service is an important part of our democracy. Military service is all I know. It has been such a major part of how I have lived my life for the past twenty years. When I decided to join military service, I did it with a plan. Anyone who is concerned about his or her future will look and see what types of options are out there. As I went through the process and saw the things I could do to live the type of life I wanted to live, have some success and feel good about myself in the process, the road led to military service. I initially wanted to do it part-time as a reservist. Once I became a part of it, I realized I was a part of something far greater than I could have imagined. My desire was then to go active duty, and I found a lot of things changed for me. One of the things was my level of commitment to serve and my patriotism. At eighteen years old, you can only be so patriotic; however, when I joined the military and realized what the Department of Defense (DOD) did and how we fit into the puzzle of what makes America great, military service was for me.

The work of the DOD and its various parts have informed my work and inspire me as I work with the Reserve Officer Training Program (ROTC). The DOD is broken down into parts, the operating force, but what we are a part of is the force generational. The ROTC is one of the branches that helps commission officers and lieutenants. There are four ways they can do it: direct commission, Officer Candidate School (OCS), Army ROTC and through the Academy. As an OCS grad, I did have at one point in time a desire to do ROTC. As a generating force, it allows the army to meet its end state years from now. The ability to see the long-term goals and responsibilities of the military is what has kept me in the army and inspires my work with the ROTC program. Being a professor of military science and being Army ROTC, I can now take the younger men and women and shape, mold and mentor them to make a greater impact than I felt I ever could. That is why I like and enjoy being a professor of military science.

Teaching military science at Howard University is something that is special to me. Today, we have the Commander's Cup, and we have the competition between air force and army named for General Howard. So on to the legacy of how we got started, from military service. For me, watching the great leaders like Togo West who have come through, I couldn't begin to name all of the alumni who have come from Howard.

Some will ask why is Howard important. I will explain in a short story. We had the opportunity to participate in a funeral service for a General Hawkins, one of our alumni who passed away. His legacy of service—taking what he learned from "Truth and Service" at Howard University and what he was able to accomplish in his career—is an inspiration to our cadets. The fact that he routinely gave back to Howard University is phenomenal. So why Howard? Because some programs do, most programs don't. What Howard does is inspire. Howard inspires those leaders to come back and contribute and do it to a level that's going to help not only Howard University military alumni but also the military's ambition to build diversity among its senior leaders.

Initially coming to service as a PMS for Howard, I understood the reputation and prestige of the university; what I didn't completely understand was the amount of commitment and dedication of the faculty, the staff, everyone coming together in order to maintain that legacy to grow the Howard brand and to contribute. In many cases, you wouldn't think that Howard would be pro-military. But I find that there are so many veterans here who just do it without having to say that they are pro-military that it's often overlooked. I was in a faculty meeting, and someone was a reservist and talked about being a reservist and the things they were doing for their part. Howard not only has a legacy but still has people in service today who are contributing and making ROTC strong. And I would not have seen that if I wasn't sitting in this seat. The office of undergraduate studies, the provost, the deans, all university departments are working to produce some of the nation's greatest leaders both within and outside of DOD service, and I am fortunate to be a part of it.

ARCHIE L. SMITH, MAJ, AV
Department Chair and Professor of Military Science
Howard University

THE AIR FORCE
AT HOWARD UNIVERSITY

The Air Force Reserve Officer Training Program at Howard University is a special program. The history of the program adds to its importance. It was one of the first AFROTC programs in the nation and began with the U.S. Air Force itself. Since that time, it has continued to support the development of the U.S. Air Force and the armed forces in general. The mission of the U.S. Air Force is to "fly, fight and win...in air, space and cyberspace." In fulfillment of this mission, the AFROTC program at Howard University greatly contributes to the development of cadets, who have high moral character, personal integrity and exhibit professionalism.

Howard University ROTC is important because of the history behind the program in addition to its contributions to the diversity of the U.S. Air Force by the officers we commission each year. Our numbers are not that big, but if you put us with the other HBCUs to increase the diversity of the armed forces, there is no other way the Department of Defense (DOD) can meet that demand. You might have three African American cadets from majority schools, but when you add up all the detachments, you might have fifty total. But when you add seven HBCUs that offer ten per year, that's seventy. As Howard is one of the original detachments, it is important to maintain that tradition.

The tradition of military service is important for the defense of our nation. Less than 1 percent of the U.S. population protects the remaining 99 percent. If you took all the services, there are probably one million of us.

It is a profession; its self-governing. We provide a service: being a deterrent to war. Some of the biggest peace lovers are those in the military. We don't necessarily want to go to war, but we are trained to go to war. We also are subject-matter experts in the art of warfare. We are trained to break things and kill people, but we don't necessarily want to do that. If called upon and diplomacy ends, the military will step in and do what it needs to do. Another part of the profession is ongoing training and having high standards. I say to some of our candidates who come in for interviews that it's great that you have the basic requirements, the GPA, SAT score and you can pass a physical test, but can you walk the walk, too?

The importance of military service is why the AFROTC continues to receive support from the university community. The support has shifted—not by intent, but by time. It is not outside of the norm for Howard as an organization to support the military. There is a lot of support, but we are building to have it more entrenched and get the word out. As we go around and speak to different student organizations and faculty, they do not have the experience of having relatives who have served in the military. Often, we are told, "Thank you for your service," but I like to reply, "Thank you for your support," because without that support, we would not be able to do what we do.

The legacy of Howard and the armed forces is in great hands with the two ROTC units on campus. With the continued support of the university community, this legacy will continue for another 150 years.

LIEUTENANT COLONEL RICHARD A. GREENLEE JR., USAF
Chairman, Department of Aerospace Studies
Commander, AFROTC Detachment 130

PREFACE

This project began with a desire to find a way to mark the sesquicentennial of Howard University. With this in mind, the idea was to celebrate Howard's role in support of the nation, specifically the military. Many of its founders were Civil War soldiers, most notably its namesake, General Oliver Otis Howard. Known as the "national negro university," Howard would obviously have a deep connection to the training of African Americans for military service. It was also clear that the stance of the university as a supporter of the African American race would mean it also had to support African American soldiers. This book tells the story of Howard University and the armed forces.

I have always been fascinated with the experience of African Americans in the military. It is a tale that mirrors the entire African American experience. Those who participated did so with pride. African Americans desired to showcase their patriotism. With that, they rose to action in an effort to prove their worth and gain equal rights for all African Americans. The desire to attain full citizenship through service is not a new concept. That African Americans participated in this action is not surprising given the history of the United States.

The project started with the digitization of letters in the Howard University Men and Women in the Armed Forces Collection in the Moorland Spingarn Research Center at Howard University (MSRC). The collection consisted of over one hundred letters Howardites sent to the university while they were serving in World War II. The letters reflect the pain, joy and pride felt by all black soldiers during their participation in the war. A selection of these letters can be found in the appendix.

The next collection to be digitized was the Prometheans Inc. The Prometheans was a group formed by Howard alumni from the Army Specialized Training Program at Howard. The group was formed while the men were serving in World War II. The collection documents the formation of the organization. It also contains letters from the soldiers detailing their experiences and their hope to support one another following the war. Other collections digitized as part of this effort include the military documents in the Thomas Montgomery Gregory Collection and the ledgers of the early Military Department at the university.

Credit for the idea for a publication must be given to Joellen Elbashir. Elbashir is the curator for manuscripts at MSRC. After a discussion about establishing a permanent way to recognize Howard's role in the military, she suggested a publication. The original idea was to publish the letters in the men and women in the armed forces collection. However, the idea to write a narrative soon overtook this.

We begin with an introduction that discusses the history of African Americans in the armed forces. This is done to provide context to the role that Howard University has played in supporting the armed forces. It begins at the American Revolution and ends with a discussion of the advances made since the end of segregation in the military. Howard University's role in this is explained in later chapters. This includes the role of Howard in the training of African American soldiers and its role in helping to desegregate the military.

Many of the sources for this book can be found on Digital Howard. This was done by design. Digital Howard is the institutional repository of the Howard University Libraries and MSRC. The institutional repository is a relatively new development in the world of archives. By completing this work using this new resource, I hope to show the viability of the repository as an important contributor to research.

The service of African Americans in the support of democracy is an important one. From the time of the American Revolution to our current fight against terrorism, African Americans have played a vital role in the defense of the nation. The role of Howard University in the fight for democracy is vital to the story of African Americans in the armed forces. While not often pleasant, the story of African Americans in the armed forces is the story of a country moving in the direction of living up to its founding ideals of freedom and justice for all. The stories of these men and women tell the story of American history. Let us not forget their sacrifice.

It is the hope of this author that by the end of this publication, the reader will have gained two things. The first is an appreciation for the hard work and sacrifice of African Americans in the armed forces. The second is knowledge of the important role of Howard University in the support of African Americans in the armed forces.

ACKNOWLEDGEMENTS

This book would not have been accomplished without the help and support of the staff of the Moorland Spingarn Research Center. Dr. Clifford Muse, Tewodros Abebe and Sonja Woods from the Howard University Archives; Joellen El Bashir, Dr. Al-Haji Conteh, Meaghan Alston and Richard Jenkins from the Manuscript Division; and Ishmael Childs and Amber Junipher from the Library Division. I would also like to thank Major Archie Smith, head of the Army ROTC, and Lieutenant Colonel Richard Greenlee, chairman, Department of Aerospace Studies, Commander, Det 130, AFROTC, at Howard University for their support. I would also be remiss if I did not acknowledge the support I received from my family, Gloria Webster, Toyette Pridget and Bertram Richardson.

AFRICAN AMERICANS
IN THE ARMED FORCES

Military service has played a major part in the history of African Americans. Since the American Revolution, there has been a black presence in the U.S. military. Despite this, African Americans were not fully welcomed into military service until recently. Nevertheless, it has provided financial stability for thousands of black families when racism and segregation limited their economic mobility. Through its status as an educational and support system for the African American community, Howard University has played a prominent role in supporting African Americans in the armed forces. This work celebrates that contribution.

African Americans have had a complicated relationship with the armed forces throughout the history of the United States. The participation of African Americans in the armed forces began with the dawning of the United States itself. With the beginning of hostilities in the American Revolution, African Americans valiantly fought for the American colonists at Lexington and Concord. However, upon organizing the Continental army, its commander George Washington forbade the enlistment of black soldiers. This was based on three fears. The first was the thought that the war would encourage those who were enslaved to leave their plantations. Leaders also feared that armed black men might turn on their compatriots in an effort to end slavery. In contradiction to this notion, they also believed that black men were too cowardly to make good soldiers.

On the other side, the British were willing to accept the help of African Americans to beat the colonists. With the announcement of freedom in exchange for service, thousands of African Americans flocked to the British side during the war. The men fought under the banner "Liberty to Slaves" and included hundreds of escaped enslaved persons from plantations across the South and some from the North. Despite this, many more offered their services to the colonists.

Those who fought for the American colonists did so for one major reason. Many were inspired by the colonial rhetoric of freedom and liberty for all. Pronouncements of "give me liberty or give me death" and speeches heralding the enlightenment ideals of the universal rights of man inspired many African Americans. These African Americans generally came from the North. While the specter of slavery did exist in the region, the ideals of human liberty were much more strongly espoused.

Realizing the success of the British army with its recruitment of black soldiers, George Washington finally relented, allowing black soldiers to enlist in December 1775. However, enlistment was limited to those who had previously fought for the colonies. Fear of alienating southern slaveholders discouraged further action. However, as we would see in later wars, the need for troops outweighed the fear of angering slaveholders. Enlistment in the Continental army was opened to all African Americans in 1776.

The success of the colonists and the establishment of the United States of America left many African Americans cautiously optimistic about their futures. For those who fought for the British, the promise of freedom from the United States was kept. Many sailed with the British army and settled in Nova Scotia, Sierra Leone or the British West Indies. Those who fought for the colonists were left with the hope that they would receive equal treatment and an end to the institution of slavery. This hope was partially fulfilled.

With the end of the American Revolution, the state of the institution of slavery was in question. It stood in stark contrast to the ideals and rhetoric of the Revolution. This led to the gradual dismantling of the institution throughout the northern states. By 1860, only a few slaves remained in the North. This was not the case in the southern region of the United States. In this area, slavery grew more entrenched.

Any discussion of African Americans and their participation in the American Revolution must include the topic of loyalty. For many African Americans who participated in the war effort did so not out of loyalty to the either group. Their support was conditional. This idea was best expressed by historian Benjamin Quarles. In his book the *Negro in the American Revolution*, he asserted, "The Negro in the revolution can best be understood by realizing that his major loyalty was not to a place nor to a people, but to a principle." Freedom and equality were those principles.[1]

African Americans again answered the call for service during the War of 1812. The war was essentially a battle between Great Britain and France for control in the Western Hemisphere. The United States was drawn into the fight after British forces began arming Native Americans in the Northwest and interfering with American shipping. A latent desire among Americans to annex Canada also contributed. When the British invaded the Mid-Atlantic, they issued a call for slaves to join their army in return for exchange for freedom. African Americans answered the call and fought with the British army that burned Washington, D.C., and attempted to take Baltimore.

Though their participation faced obstacles, African Americans also volunteered to fight for the American side in the war. By this period, racism and a fear of revolt led to African Americans being banned from participation in the armed forces in the United States. The Haitian Revolution mixed with the anxieties created by the discovery of planned slave revolts throughout the United States contributed to the fears of arming African Americans. The Militia Act of 1792 banned black participation in state militias and the secretary of the navy also banned black participation in that division. The only area to allow black participation was New York. Fearing invasion by the British, the state legislature authorized the creation of two regiments of black soldiers. In return for their service, the state offered freedom for the enslaved and compensation for their owners. Stopped at Baltimore, the British army conceded defeat, and the men never saw action.

The outbreak of the American Civil War drew African Americans to participate in the armed forces once more. African Americans jumped at the chance to participate in the Civil War for a number of reasons. One reason was that many blacks felt that the war was "a crusade for liberty." For them, the North winning the war would rid the country of slavery and eventually lead to civil rights for African Americans. Another reason was that they wanted to show "their patriotic zeal and unwavering loyalty" to the Union. This, too, was in the hope that they would eventually be accepted by whites and would gain equality. The question of African American participation was foremost on the minds of many.[2]

In the North and South, the question over whether blacks should participate was already answered for a number of whites. They believed blacks should not participate. One reason for this feeling was the commonly held belief that blacks, mostly ex-slaves, were "too servile and cowardly to make good soldiers."[3] This more than likely grew out of the subservient behavior that former slaves learned on the plantation and exhibited even after gaining freedom. Another belief was that the war would not last longer than ninety days. The racial prejudices of some of the white soldiers were another reason for white opposition to black involvement in the war. For example, Captain Felix Brannigan of the Seventy-Fourth New York Regiment is quoted in James McPherson's *The Negro's Civil War*, as having said, "We don't want to fight side and side with the nigger.... [W]e think we are too superior a race for that." Brannigan was not alone in his thinking. An article published in 1862 by the *New York Times* states, "I am not quite sure there is not one man in ten but would feel himself degraded as a volunteer if Negro equality is to be the order in the field of battle."[4]

Whites were not the only ones to oppose black participation in the Civil War; many blacks themselves did not like the idea of blacks participating in the war. Many felt that because they were not treated as citizens and not given equal protection under the law, blacks should not fight in a war for the United States. They felt that unless the oppression that blacks had to face in the United States was stopped, they should not press for (and refuse if offered) participation in the war as soldiers. In a letter to the editor of the New York–based *Anglo-African* newspaper, one man stated that "no regiments of black troops should leave their bodies to rot upon the battlefield beneath a southern sun...[T]he raising of black regiments for the war would be highly impolitic and uncalled for under the present state of affairs [and] the policy of the government in relation to the colored man." In another letter, Troy from New York concurred with the other writer and further stated that he and other Northern blacks were "in no condition to fight under the flag [that] gives us no protection." As the debate raged, blacks, many of them escaped slaves, did play roles in the war for the North and the South.[5]

Before they were allowed to be soldiers, free blacks and escaped slaves did a number of things to help in the war. White soldiers of the Union army who allowed blacks into their camps found odd jobs for them to do, sometimes even using them as their own personal servants. Blacks were also allowed into camps so that they could sell the soldiers "cakes and other dainties."[6] In the South, slaves were also put to work for the Confederate army. Blacks worked as teamsters, laborers, servants and cooks for the Confederate army. These jobs were also done by blacks in the North. Not surprisingly, the majority, if not all, of the food that was supplied to the Confederate army was grown and harvested by blacks. Blacks built many of the Confederate fortifications that were used in the war.

For the Union, allowing slaves within Federal lines was a problem for the government. Still fearful of causing the border states to secede, the War Department gave many orders telling soldiers to expel free blacks and slaves from Federal lines. The department was responding to the requests of slaveholders, mainly in Maryland, who claimed that they were not allowed to retrieve their slaves from within the camps. Major General John A. Dix wrote in August 1861 that "unless we abstain from the reception of the capture of fugitive slaves, we shall expose ourselves to the imputation of intermeddling with a matter entirely foreign to the great questions of political right and duty involved in the civil strife, which [has] been brought upon us by disloyal and unscrupulous men." Despite this feeling and the orders of their top commanders, officers continued to allow blacks into Federal lines.

In 1862, the first provisions were made for the enlistment of black soldiers in the Union army. The first was the Militia Act passed by Congress on July 17, 1862. It accomplished this by freeing slaves owned by Rebels who were enlisted in the army. To add on to the Militia Act, in October 1863, the War Department made General Order No. 329. This order "provided for the enlistment of the free blacks, slaves of disloyal owners, and slaves of consenting loyal owners in the border states." Adding to this group was the Emancipation Proclamation. While the document did not free slaves in the border states, and—as noted by many—did not legally free all those enslaved, it signaled an end to slavery. To those enslaved within the Confederacy, the Proclamation meant they were free, and they readily left their plantations and joined the Union army.

Thousands of African Americans fought for the Union forces in the Civil War. Most were free African Americans from the North. Others, as mentioned earlier, were African Americans who escaped bondage in the South. Some African Americans, notably black slaveholders, did support the Confederacy. There were even attempts to raise a black brigade in support of the Confederacy. These attempts came too late in the war, and the assembled group never saw fighting.

Fighting in the Civil War was based on the same ideals with which African Americans had always served the nation. The principles of freedom and equality were the basis for their actions. While some questioned the war's purpose, it was clear that this was the cause they were fighting for. The next war the United States entered caused some challenges for many African Americans.

The Spanish-American War began as a war for the freedom of oppressed peoples in the Spanish colonies. It was essentially a civil war, and the United

States entered the war under the auspices of assisting the colonists. The sinking of the USS *Maine* was used as the primary justification. Black soldiers showed extreme valor in fighting this war. The famed Buffalo Soldiers, a group of black soldiers, even saved the life of future U.S. president Theodore Roosevelt. Questions related to the service of black soldiers arose once the war took a precipitous turn.

As hostilities with the Spanish army came to an end, the Americans found themselves fighting the very people they claimed to be supporting. In the Philippines, the freedom fighters expected the United States to leave with the Spanish. However, the U.S. forces remained with the idea to "civilize" the people. Thus began a guerilla war against the United States. The question arose: would African Americans continue to participate in a war that had essentially become a war to subjugate other people of color? For those fighting, there was no question. Their loyalties lay with the United States, and they fully participated in hostilities until victory was declared by the United States in July 1902. Unlike in years past, African Americans were not expelled from the armed forces at the end of official hostilities, and African Americans participated in the American expedition into Mexico in 1916.

With the coming of World War I, African Americans again jumped at the chance to show their patriotism and fight for the United States. However, racism led many to be relegated to servile positions. While over 380,000 black men served during World War I, only 42,000 saw actual combat. When black men displayed their heroism and battle in combat, their accomplishments were often dismissed by their white counterparts. However, they were recognized by other countries. For example, France awarded the Croix de Guerre, its highest military honor, to the black regiments that assisted in freeing the country.

Despite the racism and discrimination experienced by black soldiers during World War I, there were some positive developments. Led by students at Howard University and supported by calls from the black press, the army commissioned the first group of African American officers. Over one thousand African Americans received commissions as officers. Despite their commissions, many were relegated to the lower ranks. When African American soldiers returned home, they faced the horror of what has been referred to as the Red Summer of 1919. The efforts of these students will be discussed in later chapters.

During the summer of 1919, African American soldiers returned from the front lines with a newfound pride, illustrated by this poem written by W.E.B. DuBois in the *Crisis* magazine:

Right: A group of African American soldiers machine gun training at Fort Belvoir, Virginia. *Courtesy of the Manuscript Division, Moorland Spingarn Research Center.*

Below: This photograph depicts African American soldiers during a break at Fort McLellan during World War I. *Courtesy of the Manuscript Division, Moorland Spingarn Research Center.*

We Return.
We return from fighting
We return fighting
Make way for Democracy! We saved it in France and by the Great Jehovah,
we will save it in the United States of America, or know the reason why.

This newfound pride and desire for a true democracy did not sit well with everyone within the United States. The summer is known as the "Red Summer" for the race riots that occurred throughout the United States during that year. Race riots happened in Houston, Texas; Chicago, Illinois; and Elaine, Arkansas. Despite returning to racial violence, many African Americans remained supportive of the United States and the armed forces.

World War II again saw African Americans rise to the challenge and support the war effort. Again, African Americans faced discrimination and racism within the military. Many high-ranking officials continued to hold the belief that black men would not make good soldiers. This attitude persisted despite the mounting evidence to the contrary. One such example came during the attack on Pearl Harbor in December 1941.

A parade for African American soldiers returning home from World War I in St. Louis.
Courtesy of the Manuscript Division, Moorland Spingarn Research Center.

Members of the Tuskegee Army Aviators. *Left to right*: Lieutenant John H. Prowell, James R. Polkenhorne, Claude B. Govan, William E. Griffin, Walter M. Downs, (*seated*) Roy Spencer and William H. Walker. *Courtesy of the Howard University Archives.*

During the Japanese attack on Pearl Harbor, as bombs were being dropped, Doris "Dorie" Miller rose to the occasion and became a shining example of the courage of black soldiers. Miller was a mess attendant on the USS *West Virginia*. He saved the life of his captain and took charge of the ship's machine gun during the attack. Miller is credited with shooting down between two and six enemy planes, and for his efforts, he was awarded the highest honor awarded by the U.S. Navy, the Navy Cross. He was then reassigned to mess duty and did not receive a promotion.

The most notable of all African American members of the armed forces during this period were the famed Tuskegee Airmen. Following their formation in January 1941, led by black officers, the men racked up an impressive record of service. This included flying over 15,000 sorties and completing 1,578 missions. The men were awarded numerous awards, including 150 Distinguished Flying Crosses.

Over one million African Americans served in the military during World War II. Many served in auxiliary units, including the engineering and transportation corps. When in service, the men performed their duties well in the face of several indignities. A glaring example of the indignities faced by African Americans is revealed when the treatment of black soldiers is

Pictured here are Tuskegee Navigators. Many of the Tuskegee Airmen originally trained at Howard University as part of its Army Specialized Training Program. *Courtesy of the Manuscript Division, Moorland Spingarn Research Center.*

compared to that of prisoners of war. On many bases, African Americans were barred from clubs and other social establishments. German and Italian prisoners of war, however, were allowed to enter these establishments.

The discrepancy in treatment also reveals itself when looking at the disciplining of black soldiers for real and imagined slights. This was most glaring in cases of alleged rape of white women by black soldiers. Relationships between black men and white women infuriated many white soldiers. When relationships were discovered, the black soldiers were often accused of rape. It was well known throughout the military and in the locations of the alleged rapes that many of the men were innocent. Military officials, however, felt that it was better to convict and execute these men rather than face the wrath of angry white soldiers.

The treatment was so egregious that the British press began printing damning exposés of the trials of black soldiers accused of rape. An example can be seen in a June 1944 article, "The Trial of a Negro Soldier," printed in the British *Tribune*. The article was a verbatim transcript of the trial. During the trial, it was revealed that evidence was found that the relationship was consensual and no rape occurred. Despite this, the soldier was convicted and executed. According to the editors, the transcription was printed "in defence [*sic*] or restoration of the dignity and equality of all individuals." They also noted that they were horrified by the frequency of such events.[7]

A guide was published by the U.S. military in an effort to teach black soldiers how not to be accused of rape. Titled "Let's Look at Rape," the document was signed "a Negro Chaplain." In the document, soldiers were advised to never leave the base without their passes. They were advised to not mingle with local women for fear that they were Nazi agents sent to cause racial strife. Finally, they were advised to avoid the use of alcohol, specifically cognac. "That cognac can get YOU into very, very bad trouble." The document appealed to the soldiers' sense of racial pride in begging them to listen, asserting that rape statistics would be used to harm the race and set back the cause of civil rights:

> *There are demagogues who will take these rape figures and use them as an argument why those basic American rights for which we have been clamoring should be denied us. "Look," they will say, "At how the American Negro soldiers raped the women of France. This proves that all Negroes are rapists and criminals. They lack self-control. Shall we turn them loose on the women of America?"*[8]

On the homefront, African Americans protested the poor treatment of African American soldiers. The National Association for the Advancement of Colored People (NAACP) and other civil rights organizations staged protests throughout the United States. Through the efforts of the black press, African Americans participated in a Double "V" Campaign. The goal of the campaign was to fight racism at home and fascism abroad. A. Phillip Randolph, president of the Brotherhood of Sleeping Car Porters, even suggested African Americans hold a march on Washington to protest the treatment of African Americans in the armed forces and the war industry. The League for Nonviolent Civil Disobedience Against Military Segregation was also created in support of the soldiers.

In response, the military offered some appeasements to African Americans. Chief among them were Howard University Law School dean William H. Hastie's appointment as "civilian aide on Negro Affairs" and the appointment of Benjamin O. Davis, the most senior African American in the armed forces, to the rank of brigadier general. The armed forces also capitulated to calls from black nurses to be allowed to join the war effort. The women, led by Mabel K. Staupers, executive director of the National Association of Colored Graduate Nurses, fought against quotas that limited black participation in the U.S. Army Nurses Corps. At the time, the corps was facing a nursing shortage and considered the idea of drafting nurses. President Franklin D. Roosevelt also issued Executive Order 8802, which called for the desegregation of the war industry and established the Fair Employment Practices Commission.

The most notable appeasement to the protests of the treatment of black soldiers was the decision by the War Department to lift the ban on African Americans enlisting in the U.S. Marine Corps. The men were trained at the segregated training facility at Montford Point, North Carolina, in 1942. Known as the Montford Point Marines, the men participated in military operations in the Pacific, most notably Iwo Jima. Doubting their fitness for battle, however, leaders in the Marine Corps relegated the majority to support units.

The military sought to use propaganda to quell criticism of its treatment of African Americans. Under the direction of Frank Capra, the military produced the film *The Negro Soldier*, highlighting the contributions of black soldiers to the armed forces. The film ignored any ill treatment of the soldiers during their service. The War Department also used famed African American boxer Joe Louis in its propaganda supporting the war. Photographs and film of the famous African American athlete in training were broadcast throughout the country. Despite these efforts, discrimination persisted in the military, and segregation in the military did not end until 1951.

The Korean War marked the first time African Americans were allowed to fight in desegregated units. The cause was threefold. In 1950, President Harry Truman issued Executive Order 9981, which called for an end to discrimination based on race, color, religion and national origin. The U.S. military also suffered heavy losses in the early days of fighting the war. Thirdly, the war was part of American efforts to win over the hearts and minds of world in its fight against the spread of communism. The treatment of African Americans was a major weak spot in this effort.

As the United States entered into the Vietnam War, the question of the recruitment and use of black soldiers never appeared. By 1969, black men accounted for 18 percent of the total armed forces. As they had in the past,

INTRODUCTION

African Americans joined the army for a myriad of reasons. The first, of course, was the draft. However, many volunteered and joined the armed forces to show their patriotism. Others joined to reap the benefits of military service, most notably in the area of education. Even during this period, education was difficult to attain for African Americans. The armed forces were still a big part of the African American experience.

In the years since the Vietnam War, African Americans have seen their fortunes within the armed forces reach new heights. Several African Americans were appointed as generals in the armed forces. In 1977, Clifford Alexander Jr. was appointed the first African American secretary of the army. Colin Powell has served in numerous positions, including national security advisor, commander of the U.S. Army Forces Command and chairman of the Joint Chiefs of Staff.

The history of African Americans in the armed forces is a paradox. African Americans were the subject of horrific treatment throughout the history of the United States. This included three hundred years of slavery and one hundred years of terror through racism, segregation and laws that controlled their entire lives. Despite this, African Americans remained committed to their country and served it faithfully.

HOWARD UNIVERSITY
IN THE SERVICE OF DEMOCRACY

THE ARMED FORCES AND HOWARD UNIVERSITY

The armed forces and Howard University have been intertwined since the beginnings of the university. The university's namesake, General Oliver Otis Howard, was a graduate of West Point and a Civil War hero. Many of the early leaders of the university—General Oliver Otis Howard, Silas L. Loomis, James B. Johnson, George W. Balloch, John A. Cole, Joseph A. Sladen, Eliphalet Whittlesey, Robert Reyburn, Joseph Tabler Johnson, Alexander T. Augusta, Gideon Palmer, Charles B, Purvis, Neil F. Graham, J.G. Baxter, Albert G. Riddle and Charles Howard—were former soldiers. These men instilled military life and discipline into the early life of the university. With this history, Howard University has supported the armed forces and African American soldiers in every way it could.

One of the first departments organized at the university was the Military Department. The Military Department was responsible for military-style training and the physical education of all male students at the university. Despite the military spirit of the founders, the department was short-lived. The department functioned for only three years, 1869 to 1872. The military spirit, however, did not end with the closure of the military department. A full discussion of the Military Department can be found in a later chapter.

THE COMING OF THE GREAT WAR

With the assassination of Archduke Ferdinand in Austria-Hungary, the world was plunged into World War I. The United States did not immediately enter the war. In fact, President Woodrow Wilson campaigned on the promise of keeping the United States out of the war. However, as fate would have it, the United States was forced to enter the conflict in 1917. Despite Howard's lack of a dedicated department, the coming of World War I brought the military spirit back to the university.

In March 1917, a program was held in the Andrew Rankin Chapel on campus to allow students to share their thoughts on the war and the level of support they should provide. The prevailing attitude was one of patriotism and willingness to serve their nation. The program included a speech by Sergeant D. Farrior of the famed Buffalo Soldiers' Tenth Cavalry, who recounted tales of the Battle of Carrizal and the overwhelming determination of black soldiers. At the end of the program, the group unanimously endorsed a letter written by Howard President Stephen Newman to President Woodrow Wilson declaring their support.[9] It stated:

March 20, 1917.

Dear President Wilson:

We, officers, teachers and students of Howard University, because of our unfailing devotion to our country, do hereby offer ourselves to her in mind, body and estate for whatever use she may be able to make of us in maintaining her integrity and her high position among the nations of the world.

—President Stephen M. Newman[10]

Howard's connection to the federal government is listed as a major inspiration for this support. In the *Howard University Journal*, an editorial expressed the mood, saying that "everyone from the president to the students is ready to go to the support of the government. We are ready to serve our country in any capacity. We are willing to sacrifice our lives for the honor and integrity of this democracy."[11]

The faculty and staff of the university supported the war effort financially. The group collectively bought $142,850 in liberty loan bonds. The group also financially supported other groups that supported the war effort. The Howard Community contributed $2,256 to the United War Work Campaign, Young Men's Christian Association (YMCA), Young Women's Christian Association (YWCA), Knights of Columbus and the Salvation Army. Under the leadership of Howard trustee Jesse E. Moorland, Howard men and women also supported the YMCA by traveling to camps throughout the world to provide support.[12]

Back on the campus, Howard's new president Stanley Durkee turned the entire university toward supporting the war effort in 1918. Under his direction, the university was almost completely turned into a war camp. The curriculum was changed to reflect an emphasis on war. The campus was also rebuilt to reflect this status. Four barracks were also erected on the campus. Trenches were dug, sentinels were built and armed guards were placed at the gates of the campus. To complete the transformation, soldiers were quartered in dorms and university buildings.[13]

Black soldiers in France during World War I, circa 1917. Many black soldiers were surprised how well they were treated outside of the United States. *Courtesy of the National Archives and Records Administration.*

War bond drive at Howard University *Courtesy of the Howard University Archives.*

As the university became a training ground for soldiers, the students set out to ensure that black soldiers would be able to serve in higher-ranked positions. At the urging of Howard trustee Joel Spingarn, students from Howard led the charge in convincing the War Department to train African Americans as officers in the military. Due entirely to racism, in previous wars, African Americans were banned from being trained as officers. According to Secretary of War Newton D. Baker, the training of black officers was "inadvisable" and "impracticable."

Once mobilized, the students formed an organization known as the Central Committee of Negro College Men. While led by Howard students, membership in the organization was extended to black students of several other universities. Students from Lincoln, Union, Columbia, Harvard, Yale and Brown Universities joined the movement. Support from the university was strong. The thirty-two students leading the movement were allowed to take a leave of absence from their coursework to focus on their work.[14]

Pressure from the students resulted in the War Department establishing the first officer training school for African Americans in the nation, the Seventeenth Provisional Training Camp in Des Moines, Iowa. According to an article in the *Howard University Catalog*, the program was started "as a result of the extraordinary enthusiasm, resourcefulness, race loyalty, and patriotism exhibited by the students of Howard." In the *Howard University Journal*, the Howard students' success at the camp was described. The authors stated with the utmost modesty, "Howard men are conspicuous not only for their numbers and good looks, but for their enthusiasm tempered with self-control, their genial adaptability and scholarly attainment." More importantly, they recognized the gravity of the enlistees' actions: "Honor is due to all men at Fort Des Moines who have done their very best to prove the lie to the pernicious theory of racial inequality with equal opportunity, whether or not they succeed in realizing their personal ambition." Some 200 students and faculty members from Howard were trained at the camp—95

African American soldiers at Fort McLellan standing at attention during World War I. *Courtesy of the Manuscript Division, Moorland Spingarn Research Center.*

Howardite Thomas Montgomery
Gregory (*right*) poses with fellow
soldier holding bayonets during
World War I. *Courtesy of the Howard
University Archives.*

of this group received commissions. In total, 1,250 men were trained at the
camp and 659 received commissions.[15]

Howard University itself also developed a program for the training
of African American soldiers. The university opened a Student Army
Training Camp (SATC) to support their training. In November 1917,
the university also opened a radio school. Over three hundred men from
the District of Columbia were trained and received certificates from the
school. While these programs were restricted to men, female students were
not ignored.[16]

Although they were not allowed to participate in formal military
training, the female students at the university found ways to support the
war effort. A unit of the Circle for Negro War Relief was established. An
American Red Cross unit was formed on the campus in March 1917. The
officers of the group were Hallie E. Queen, chairman; Edna Brown, vice-
chairman; Esther Shackleford, steward; Dorothy Pelham, assistant steward;
Cavassa Satter White, treasurer; Jennie Baer, Annie R. Barker, Nannie
Board, Elsie Brown, Ruth Freeland Rosabelle Jernagin, Sadye Martin,
Etta Morton, Adelaide Smith, Mary Waring and Gladys Washington,
group captains.[17]

At the time, African American women were not allowed to serve as Red Cross nurses. As a result, they settled on volunteering for the sewing unit. This restriction did not damper their enthusiasm. Queen stated, "We shall give our time and energy gladly, for we feel that in our sewing, though our needle weapon is a simple, homely one, we are preforming a real and necessary service for America."[18] The restriction meant their activities were limited to raising funds to support the war effort and knitting over one thousand garments to send to the soldiers. The women also formed a Girls Battalion in 1918. Two companies of young women were developed. The groups participated in drilling, battalion reviews and drill competitions.[19]

At the conclusion of the war effort, the university slowly returned to normal. Regular classes resumed, and students returned to regular coursework. The SATC was demobilized in December 1918 after having trained 1,786 men. Following the demobilization, the university developed

Memorial tablet commemorating the Student Army Training Camp and the service of Howard University. It was presented by Professor Alain Locke, chairman of the Negro Student Army Association, November 12, 1919. *Courtesy of the Howard University Archives.*

The instructors for the Student Army Training Corps on the campus of Howard Universtiy. *Courtesy of the Howard University Archives.*

Members of the SATC train on the yard on the Howard University campus, 1917. *Courtesy of the Howard University Archives.*

the Reserve Officer Training Corps. This program was arguably the first such group established at a black school. Participation in the program was compulsory for all "physically fit" male students. It was through the ROTC that Howard's support for the armed forces remained until the outbreak of World War II.

Organizing in Support of World War II

Much like it had during World War I, the university developed a number of initiatives to support the war effort during World War II. It was clear to many at the university that the war was a just cause. Tales of the vehement racism and atrocities committed by Adolf Hitler and his Nazi regime were well known to many in the United States. Howard itself became a place of refuge, as it helped Jewish professors in Germany escape the Holocaust and provided them with teaching positions. The university again mobilized in the service and defense of democracy and freedom.

In 1940, Howard president Mordecai Johnson established the University-Wide Committee on Education and National Defense. The role of this committee was to investigate and implement programs to support the war effort. Leading the committee was then university secretary James M. Nabrit Jr. Through the work of this committee, the university's curriculum was changed to reflect the ongoing crisis.

During 1940–41 school year, the University-Wide Committee on Education and National Defense developed a series of lectures to teach students about the war and how it affected them. The general theme of the lectures was "The Negro in the Present World Crisis." Faculty members from across the university were tapped to provide the lectures. Each group was asked to adapt the theme to its respective field. The goal was to provide a complete picture of the crisis and how it affected all aspects of life both civilian and military, abroad and on the homefront.

With the support of the committee, departments across the campus developed their own curriculums around the war effort. Through the College of Liberal Arts, a course titled "Orientation Lecture Series: The Basis of the Present Conflict" was offered to the entire university community. All military personnel on the campus were ordered to take the course. The Department of Psychology developed the course "Psychology of Modern Warfare." The course covered the "selection of military personnel; civil and military morale; psychology of propaganda; war neuroses." The Department of History developed the course "Europe Since 1931." The class was "an analysis of the world crisis and its effects cultural, economic, political, social, intellectual." The School of Religion also offered a course that discussed the effects of the war on society, "Christianity and the World Community." This course examined "prevailing and anticipated obstacles to the establishment of world community in the post-war era. The bearing of applied Christianity upon these and the possibilities for Christian institutions in furthering their solution comprise the perspective from which the problems will be viewed."[20]

The School of Engineering and Architecture developed an Engineering Defense Training Program to support the war effort. The defense courses developed under the program were provided tuition-free and taught in the evenings to increase their availability. The program was soon replaced by the Engineering, Science and Management Defense Training Program sponsored by the U.S. Office of Education. Over six hundred students were enrolled in the program. Courses taught through the program included architectural drafting, basic principles of organic chemistry, chemistry of powder and explosives, geodetic computer and surveying and mapping.[21]

The university also shifted its calendar to support and accelerate training. The semesters were again switched to the quarter system. The benefits of the quarter system were especially necessary to support the members of the armed forces. Under this system, the four-year course of study could be completed in three years. Following this system meant that many of the soldiers trained at the university were able to enter the service with college degrees. With degrees, they were able to qualify for higher forms of service.[22]

The university also established the University Center for Civilian Morale Service. The purpose of the service was to carry out activities throughout the District of Columbia. The community developed a library of literature on the war and related issues. The center also developed forums, lectures and discussions around the war effort. Leadership also facilitated "cooperative relations" between organizations in the District of Columbia.[23]

The university was very active in the area of civil defense and developed a number of subcommittees to support the cause. A committee was created for the Air Raid Warden Service. This committee divided the campus into north and south zones for the purposes of preparing for air raids.

In addition, a committee on military service problems was created. This committee focused on providing support to individuals who experienced problems with selective service, getting information related to volunteering or accessing benefits.[24]

The university also created a subcommittee on women in national defense. This committee conducted surveys and developed events that allowed women to participate in the war effort. Their greatest success came in the development of campaigns to support the soldiers. Campaigns included books for soldiers, clothing drives for refugees, the sale of war stamps and bonds and promoting conservation. In the area of conservation, the university also created a subcommittee on conservation of cultural resources. Under the leadership of Dr. Walter G. Daniel, the university developed a plan to preserve its historic rare books, documents and other valuable historical artifacts in the case of attack.[25]

The university was fully committed to supporting the war effort. This included financial support. The university purchased $8,586.25 worth of defense bonds and $1,579.70 of defense stamps by April 1942. The university also pledged to purchase an additional $1,671 worth of stamps and bonds a month during the war. Considering the usually unstable financial condition of the university, this commitment was a big step.[26]

The support of the war effort by the university and its employees was not limited to on campus functions. Several members of the university community participated in national efforts to support the United States in the war. President Johnson was a member of the National Committee on Defense of the American Council on Education. Dr. Charles H. Thompson, dean of the College of Liberal Arts, joined the Wartime Commission of the U.S. Office of Education and the Sub-Committee on Education, Joint Army and Navy Committee on Recreation and Welfare. Dr. Ralph Bunche, chairman of the Department of Political Science, was appointed head of the subdivision on Africa and Native Affairs in the British Empire Section of the Office of the Coordinator of Information. Dr. Rayford Logan of the Department of History conducted a special study of Latin American relations as it related to the war for the Office of Inter-American Affairs. Physics professor Frank Coleman and James Nabrit served on Draft Board No. 12 for Washington, D.C., with Coleman acting as chair. Law school professor Dr. George M. Johnson also participated as assistant executive secretary of the President's Committee on Fair Employment Practice. Many other faculty members contributed to the war efforts through the support of various other organizations.[27]

The most prolific of Howard faculty to support the war effort was Dr. Charles R. Drew, head of the Department of Surgery. He is credited with savings millions of lives through his work with blood plasma. In 1940, Dr. Drew was medical supervisor of the Blood Plasma Division, Blood Transfusion Association, New York, in charge of the collection of blood plasma for the British army. He later became assistant director of blood procurement of the National Research Council, in charge of collection of blood for use by the U.S. Army and Navy. Drew resigned from service, however, after a ruling by the War Department called for the segregation of African American blood donations.[28]

Outside of its official work, the university provided a larger service in the support of the war effort by providing moral support to the Howard students and alumni fighting in the war. The university sent many letters and care packages to alumni. Many of the students replied, sharing their joy at being thought of and their happy thoughts of Howard. Their thoughts and feelings about Howard and the experiences they shared with the university will be discussed in a later chapter.

RECOGNIZING THE MEN FOR THEIR SERVICE

In March 1941, the theme of the Annual Charter Day exercises was "Howard University in the Service of a Democracy." In choosing the theme, the university wanted to highlight its role in the "workings of democracy." The leadership also wanted to highlight the role the university would play in the future of the United States. Charter Day events each focused on a different aspect of the university's service to the United States.

With the theme of service, the university hosted several events around the campus. Dr. Charles H. Garvin delivered a presentation on "The Negro Doctor, Past and Present." Garvin was president of the Cleveland Library Board, assistant surgeon in urology at Lakeside Hospital, Cleveland, Ohio; and clinical instructor in genitourinary surgery at the Western Reserve University School of Medicine. On behalf of Alpha Kappa Alpha sorority, the group's president, Dr. Dorothy Boulding-Ferebee, presented the table on which the original deed of the university was signed.[29]

During the exercises, a tribute was also paid to Howard president Mordecai W. Johnson. The event was organized by the Howard Board of Trustees in honor of Johnson's fifteen years as president of the university.

Federal Security Administrator Paul V. McNutt said of Johnson, "The real and everlasting results of his leadership will flow from the lives of the thousands of men and women who have passed through these halls and taken up positions of trust in the widespread communities of this country."

In his speech, Johnson outlined the role Howard University would play in support of the development of the black race. Johnson, a prolific speaker, often spoke of the role the university should play in advancing the race. This feeling contributed to his shift from his opposition to the ROTC on campus. It also led to his steadfast support of black soldiers during World War II.

At the Charter Day dinner, ROTC officers served as hosts. They were assisted by "attractive coed hostess[es]." The keynote address was given by McNutt. In his speech, McNutt addressed the important role of black leadership and Howard University. He noted that it was incumbent upon African American leaders to advance the cause of their race. Of African American leaders, he stated:

> *I am aware that the Negro leader has a particularly delicate and difficult task—as have the leaders of any so-called minority group. If he values his integrity, he must be true to his own constituents and shape his course toward advancing their cause. At the same time, he is a citizen of a larger and more all-inclusive Nation to which he owes loyalty and whose interests he must consider without falling into the error of fawning subserviency [sic] or spineless truckling. He must steer a true course or he will, on the one hand, lose the trust of his own people or, on the other hand, lose his influence in the larger commonwealth. The final test of such a leader is whether or not he can get things done which contribute to the genuine welfare of his followers rather than to his own personal aggrandizement. All the elements of statesmanship are required for success in such a task.*[30]

Similarly, he stated it was crucial that African American universities support the development of this leadership. McNutt placed a particular level of importance on Howard University:

> *Howard University is in a peculiarly important position with respect to these future leaders. This is a genuinely national university, and here is to be found the most completely rounded offering of training. You have the only Negro law school; one of two accredited medical schools; schools of engineering, dentistry and religion; departments of music and education; a magnificent library; and other departments usually found in colleges. Here*

Philip Murray, CIO president; Zora Neale Hurston, writer; and Major T.L. Hungate, alumni achievement award recipients at the 1941 Charter Day dinner honoring Howard and the military. *Courtesy of the Howard University Archives.*

> *a student can come and get acquainted with almost any phase of our culture in which he is interested. This well-rounded, well-built, and well-staffed university is a symbol of the national concern with an intelligent Negro leadership. The businessmen, the lawyers, the doctors, the teachers trained here are the return to the Nation for its investment in Howard University, and it is our concern that that return shall be of the highest quality and the maximum value.*

McNutt also discussed the work that the federal government was doing to advance the cause of the African American race. He placed particular importance on the work of Mary McLeod Bethune and the National Youth Administration. Through this program, he saw the lives of African Americans as a whole being improved through job creation. This extended to the war industry. He stressed that the inclusion of all groups within the United States was necessary for a successful nation.[31]

While celebrating the seventy-fifth anniversary of the university, the theme of race and the need to end segregation in the military and the war industry was also on display at the March 1942 Charter Day festivities. As usual with the Charter Day exercises, the event celebrated the contributions of Howard to the nation. For example, a lecture was given by Professor Walter Dyson, author of *Howard University, The Capstone of Negro Education*. However, the necessity to provide equal rights to African Americans was present.

The necessity of equal rights—particularly as a result of the work of African Americans in the military—was central to the theme of the Charter Day dinner. The event's keynote speaker was Senator Alben William Barkley, the majority leader of the U.S. Senate. Barkley spoke of the importance of equal rights and of Howard University to the education system. While his remarks focused on those African Americans in the armed forces, they reflected the idea that the rewards of hard work should extend to their fellow man.

In addressing the issue of race and the war effort, Barkley stated: "We must recognize that without designations of race, color, or religion.... [M]en compelled to fight or who volunteer to fight to preserve our national integrity and our individual liberties are entitled to work whenever their capacity and their opportunities may come together." He added:

> *We must recognize that every child born into the world has a right to a fair chance to live amid healthy and wholesome surroundings, to be educated according to his ability to absorb it, and to strive in a world of peace and justice to improve his individual as well as the collective welfare of all the people. We must recognize that men who are required to support the government with their energies, with their earnings or their blood, have a right to a fair share and a fair voice in determining the kind of government which they and their fellow men shall life under.*[32]

As the war continued, the university continued to recognize the students pulled into wartime service. In 1943, the university held a special chapel service dedicated to the students leaving for the war that semester. Sixty-five men from the ROTC program entered the service in that semester. The program was led by dean of the chapel Dr. Howard Thurman and included remarks by Beatrice Turner, editor of the *Hilltop* student newspaper; Lewis Giles of the ROTC; Dr. J. St. Clair Price for the faculty; and Mordecai Johnson, university president. The glee club also performed.[33]

HOWARDITES IN WAR

With their support of the war effort, Howard University students and faculty were, of course, active participants in the struggle against the Axis powers of Germany, Italy and Japan. Following the bombing of Pearl Harbor, Howardites went into action. Immediately after the attack, 150 of them went into active duty. Soon thereafter, Howard had more than 3,000 students and alumni actively participating in military service. It has been said that over 90 percent of all African American officers who participated in the war were Howard students. The faculty, students and alumni of Howard University led the charge of African American participation in the war.[34]

Through their leadership and initiative, Howardites found themselves in all areas of the armed forces during World War II. According to university records, the list of Howardites in the military included in the army 277 lieutenants, 107 captains, 19 cadets, 17 majors, 9 lieutenant colonels, 4 warrant officers, 4 nurses, 7 WACS and 2 colonels. In the navy, 27 Howardites were active, with 1 ensign and 1 lieutenant; 3 were active in the Coast Guard. The majority of the female Howardites who participated in the war were part of support units, the nursing corps and, most notably, the American Red Cross. They were actively involved in battle despite the discrimination and prejudice they faced in the towns where bases were located and sometimes on the installations themselves.[35]

Howard faculty members were also actively involved in the war effort as well. A list of Howard professors on active duty was published in the university's catalogue in 1945. They were: Louis Thomas Achille, associate professor of Romance languages; James W. Butcher Jr., instructor in English; Madison Spencer Briscoe, instructor in bacteriology; Dr. Hyman Y. Chase, associate professor of zoology; Dr. Theodore R. Corprew, clinical instructor in obstetrics; Count Kai DeVermond, instructor in voice; Sylvannus H. Hart III, instructor in brasswind and woodwind instruments; Dr. Phillip Thomas Johnson, clinical associate professor of orthopedic surgery; Dr. Cervera R. Little, clinical assistant in surgery; Dr. John Lovell Jr., assistant professor of English; W. Robert Ming Jr., associate professor of law; Dr. Theodore Pinckney, clinical instructor in orthopedic surgery; Dr. Hildrus A. Poindexter, professor of bacteriology, preventive medicine and public health; Dr. Frederick Payne Watts, assistant professor of psychology; Ernest R. Welch, associate professor of electrical engineering; and Luis Andres Wheatley, assistant in piano.[36]

Members of the 332nd Fighter Group attending a briefing in Ramitelli, Italy, March 1945. *Courtesy of the Library of Congress.*

Howardites were stationed at bases all over the world. As part of the 92nd Division and the 366th Infantry, most began their service stationed at Fort Huachuca, Arizona. Other Howardites were stationed at Fort Devens in Massachusetts; Camp Lee, Virginia; and Fort Jackson, South Carolina, among others. They served in the European, African and Pacific theaters

African American soldiers marching in Cascina, Italy. Many of the soldiers from Howard spent time serving in Italy. *Courtesy of the Manuscript Division, Moorland Spingarn Research Center.*

Black female yeomen from the U.S. Navy. Many African American women supported the military in support roles. *Courtesy of the Manuscript Division, Moorland Spingarn Research Center.*

African American nurses at Fort Bragg. Led by Mabel K. Staupers, black nurses from Freedmen's Hospital on the campus of Howard University and from around the country joined the military to provide support for black servicemen. *Courtesy of the Manuscript Division, Moorland Spingarn Research Center.*

of operation. At least sixty-seven Howardites were members of the famed Tuskegee Airmen. These men are famous for successfully completing thousands of missions, never losing an aircraft they were guarding and receiving hundreds of awards for their courage and valor.[37]

FROM SUPPORTING THE WAR EFFORT TO SUPPORTING THE SOLDIER

Despite the zeal for military service and support for the African Americans fighting in the war, there were some sobering voices on campus. In his opening convocation address in December 1944, Lester B. Granger, executive secretary of the National Urban League, warned the audience against believing that any wartime gains would be lasting for African Americans:

The "America First Movement" and all other isolationist, subversive or traitorous movements have broken up and disappeared, or have been silenced and forced underground.... There were negroes who were misled by wartime racial gains to the point of feeling that the longer the war lasted, the more secure became the situation of Negroes....[S]uch talk has disappeared, except among the ranks of the purblind and the incredibly mean and selfish....[T]here have been advances, and there have been losses. The advances have been made in the face of frequently bitter opposition that has destroyed proper appreciation of such gains as can be recorded. The losses have been suffered under conditions that contribute the utmost of humiliation and resentment to the thinking of Negro Americans.[38]

The end of World War II brought many sobering thoughts, but like many African Americans, the faculty, staff and students at Howard soldiered on. As thousands of African American veterans returned home from the front, Howard University rose to the challenge of supporting them. To this end, the university opened an office specifically to support returning veterans. Placed in Douglass Hall, the Veterans Counseling

This group of veterans is relaxing after classes with Howard students. After the war, Howard provided a training program for returning veterans. *Courtesy of the Howard University Archives.*

and Advisory Service was directed by Carroll L. Miller, a counselor in the College of Liberal Arts. The office provided support in the areas of education and personal issues.[39]

Returning veterans were supported by two laws passed by Congress. Public Law No. 16 provided funds for training disabled veterans. The Department of Veterans Affairs covered a full four years of tuition and paid a living allowance of at least $92 a month. The second law supporting the education of veterans was Public Law No. 346. This law (more popularly known as the G.I. Bill) provided for up to four years of educational training for veterans under the age of twenty-five.[40]

A large number of veterans entered the university to continue or begin their studies after the passage of the two bills. By the spring of 1947, 2,390 veterans were enrolled at Howard. The majority were enrolled in the College of Liberal Arts and College of Engineering and Architecture. Many of the veterans received training in engineering during the war, so it is clear why this was a popular field. Under PL 16, 180 veterans joined the university.[41]

ENROLLMENT OF VETERANS FOR THE YEARS 1946–47

School	Spring 1946	Autumn 1946	Winter 1946	Spring 1947
Liberal Arts	521	1483	1499	1615
Social Work	5	17	17	16
Religion	2	10	11	15
Engineer & Arch	82	341	337	332
Music	20	55	56	60
Pharmacy	26	63	66	68
Graduate	23	58	56	55
Dental	28	65	65	64
Medicine	31	107	107	107
Law	23	59	58	58
Total	761	2258	2272	2390

Veterans attending engineering class on aviation at Howard University, 1946. *Courtesy of the Howard University Archives.*

To support the veterans, students at the university formed the American Veterans Committee. The group was made up of veterans of World War II. The motto for the group was "Citizens first, veterans second." The goal of this group was to provide further support to students who were veterans. Combined with the efforts of the Veterans Counseling and Advisory Service, the group did much to support the reintegration of veterans back into society and university life. The university also facilitated support for returning veterans who were alumni of the university.[42]

THE PROMETHEANS

Supporting one another as Howard alumni did not end after hostilities ended. During the war, a group of Howard alumni joined together to form the Prometheans. The purpose of the group was to support Howard alumni who were in the service transition to successful civilian lives. One of the important services provided by the organization at the time of its founding was contact information for the men. In later years, the organization provided meetings and events for the men to reconnect. The Prometheans was one of the most enduring legacies of Howard's support of the war effort.

The Prometheans Club, as it was known, was formed at Fort Huachuca, Arizona. Many Howard alumni were stationed at this installation at some point during their military service. Members of the club were gathered from the 2515th SU Army Specialized Training Program at Howard University. The name Prometheans was special to the men and signified the purpose of the group. The Greek god Prometheus represented light and power. For the former members of the 2515th, "light and power" was what they wanted to provide to their membership, with the stated goal of providing support as they transitioned to civilian life. The organization was to be "a guiding light and guiding power for the men in the ASTP at Howard University."[43]

The original leaders of the group were Burrell DeHaven, chairman; Corporal Hobart Turner and Private James Butler managed publicity and supply; T/5 John G. Smith and Private Marion Poole handled information; and Private First Class David Cason, Private Robert C. Morris and Private First Class Carl Slaughter managed correspondence. Leadership was further divided by "major units" and "minor units" within the major units. Each unit was to have a sergeant at arms and secretary. This was done to ensure that while the men were dispersed they were still able to come together as a group.[44]

Understanding that they would be dispersed to the various fronts of the war, the men had the foresight to establish a permanent base of operations. It was decided that Howard University would be the seat for the organization. To manage the organization at Howard, the group chose Dr. Merze Tate, Lieutenant Colonel Raymond Contee, Dr. Herman Branson, Dr. Dudley Woodard and Professor John Hughuley to lead. The group managed correspondence, maintained a directory and collected dues for the organization.[45]

Dr. Merze Tate was a fitting person to manage an organization supporting Howard alumni in the military. Tate was the first woman to earn a doctoral degree in government and international relations from Harvard. She also was one of the first women to join the History Department at Howard. Her research and publications on disarmament

Howard University, ASTP basic engineering student, circa 1940. *Courtesy of the Howard University Archives.*

and the military made her uniquely suited to lead such efforts. In this role, Tate acted as the coordinator for the organization. She ensured that the group received recognition and support from the wider university community. This included corresponding with the university's president Mordecai W. Johnson to establish a memorial. Although the original idea never came to fruition, there is a plaque commemorating the group located at the flagpole on the yard, or main quadrangle.

Managing the organizations funds also was the responsibility of Dr. Tate. The group collected dues for the purpose of developing a fund that would financially support members in need following the war. This fit perfectly with the organization's mission of being a light to help members after leaving the service. Outside of this, the organization also used the funds to support the war effort. The group purchased a bond in the Howard University seventh war bond drive.[46]

With the support of the Veterans Counseling and Advisory Service at Howard, Tate also produced a newsletter for the organization. Included in the newsletters were updates on the various members and articles that the men would find interesting. For example, one newsletter featured a discussion on the views of white officers and sergeants in the European theater of operations who managed platoons of black soldiers. The article included answers to a survey of 250 men who served with black soldiers. When asked before working with the men if they were skeptical of their performance, over 60 percent said they felt apprehensive about working with the black soldiers, but 70 percent noted that after working with the soldiers, their opinion of them increased dramatically. None reported opinions decreasing. When asked to rate the African Americans' performance, all of the respondents rated them as doing "very well" or "fairly well."[47]

Information of this kind was significant for the soldiers. At the beginning of the war, military leaders were apprehensive about allowing African American soldiers to participate in combat units. Dating to the American Revolution, military leaders doubted the fitness of African Americans as soldiers. In every instance, when black soldiers were allowed to participate, they rose to the occasion and performed admirably. Understanding that this was how they would be viewed, knowing that their performance was being noticed and highly rated provided a boost of morale.

Also included in the newsletters were correspondence sent by soldiers giving updates on location, families and other general information. They also included notes encouraging the soldiers to remain in contact and to be successful upon their return. In his letter, Burrell DeHaven implored the men to be active: "You are the 'tomorrow' so it is your duty to preserve the peace that has been won." In announcements, the bulletins included updates highlighting the work of the soldiers and announcing their return from overseas. An example of this can be found in the announcement for Promethean Nathanial Pruitt. Upon his return from the front, the newsletter announced that he was finally retiring from the service after having served in World War I and II. It detailed the medals Pruitt received for service in each war and the locations of his service. In keeping with the theme of providing support, Tate also shared job announcements for the soldiers. The production of the newsletters continued for many years following the end of the war.[48]

One of the benefits derived from the Prometheans was a service to help the servicemen find their compatriots. As seen in many letters from alumni, the ability to maintain contact with their fellow service members was important to the men. The Prometheans provided contact information for Howard alumni in the service. Sergeant Byron Turnquest requested use of this service during his time overseas. In a letter to Dr. Tate, he noted how much he missed his "buddies" from the Ninety-Second Squadron. He praised the group for not being like other groups that did not provide any real services to the soldiers. He then requested the contact information for another soldier with whom he wished to stay in touch.[49]

After the war, the group undertook many activities to remain in contact. In 1960, members formed a nonprofit organization and named themselves Prometheans Inc. The group started having formal meetings in 1968. Through this organization, the Prometheans developed a series of community service events to support African American youth. Many programs supported education and helped youth find jobs. The Prometheans also sponsored a scholarship fund for graduating seniors at Howard. In the 1970s, the group developed an emergency loan fund for Vietnam veterans attending Howard.[50]

The organization's elaborate reunions were some of its most important activities. In 1971, the group held the reunion in Dallas, Texas. The weeklong program was followed by a five-day tour of Mexico.[51] The group's thirty-first reunion was held in Chicago in 1974. The event was a joyous occasion and an example of the types of festivities held by the group. At the reunion, there was a fashion show, a dance and a tour of the city.[52]

Prometheans Inc. dissolved in 2011 for several reasons. The main reason was the age and size of its membership. By this point, there were only twenty-five members left living. Of those, many were at or nearing ninety years old. They also struggled with recruiting new members. In August, the Prometheans held their last meeting in Silver Spring, Maryland. At the event, Lute Smith implored the men and their family members to stay in touch, He said, "Friendship never dies, it just fades

Many of the Howardites in the military served with the Ninety-Second Division. In this photograph, the Fifth Army of the Ninety-Second Division sees action three miles north of Lucca, Italy, September 7, 1944. *Courtesy of the Manuscript Division, Moorland Spingarn Research Center.*

away, keep this going. Go ahead and continue this by building a legacy of friendship."[53]

The connection facilitated by the Prometheans Club is one of the organization's lasting legacies. It demonstrated the bonds that Howardites who served in the military developed. It also reflected the support provided by the university to support its veterans. With the support of the Howard faculty and staff, the veterans continued to receive support following the war. Through their efforts, the lives of these men were markedly improved and supported.

As it had done in years past, the Howard University community did all it could to support both the war effort and African American veterans. Through the University-Wide Committee on Education and National Defense, the university turned its entire focus toward supporting the war effort and black soldiers. At the close of the war, the community turned its eye toward providing support for the veterans who returned to

The Prometheans at their twentieth anniversary celebration. *Courtesy of the Howard University Archives.*

the university. Through the Veterans Counseling and Advisory Service, the university provided support for the veterans' educational as well as personal needs. Through groups such as the Prometheans, the university supported its veteran alumni.

Vietnam: The Military Spirit Begins to Wane

As the decades passed, the university's support of war efforts began to wane. The turbulence of the 1960s and the controversy that surrounded the Vietnam War meant that Howard would not engage itself in activities seen in wars past. Students at the university actively protested against the Vietnam War. The student body held a Vietnam Week in 1967, sponsored by the United Christian Campus Fellowship. The protest was held the week of April 15 to correspond with the Mobilization for Peace in Vietnam protest at the United Nations Headquarters in New York. Following the week of events on campus, over one hundred students and faculty traveled to New York to attend the event. A week later, Muhammad Ali was brought to the campus by the Black Power Committee. Addressing a crowd of two thousand in front of Douglass Hall, Ali shared with students that he would not participate in the Vietnam War and the beliefs of Islam.[54]

Compulsory ROTC also took a hit during the decade. Students spent the better part of the decade protesting the requirement, leading to its removal. As ROTC became voluntary, it ushered in a new era of the relegation of the armed forces to a smaller portion of university life. As we will see in the next chapter, the university continued to support the armed forces mainly through its ROTC program.

MILITARY EDUCATION AND TRAINING
AT HOWARD UNIVERSITY

The influence of the armed forces was felt at Howard University from its founding. As mentioned earlier, several of the founders of the university were ex-soldiers. General Oliver Otis Howard—the namesake of Howard University and head of the Bureau of Refugees, Freedmen and Abandoned Lands, commonly known as the Freedmen's Bureau—was a Civil War hero. Historian Walter Dyson described the initial organization of the university as resembling the military. Upon his appointment as the third president of Howard, General Howard began the Military Department at Howard University. Formal military instruction had come to the school.

Organization of the Military Department began on August 1, 1869. The department was developed by the Military Committee, which consisted of General Howard, D.W. Anderson and Henry A. Brewster. Through their hard work, the department was announced on September 21, 1869. The participants were known as the "Howard University Cadets." The group was led by Commandant Captain Melville C. Wilkinson. Officers were selected from among the student body and were chosen for their "military aptitude, general deportment and proficiency in studies."[55]

Participation was compulsory, and all "physically eligible" male students were to present themselves following admission. Students were required to purchase a uniform costing twelve to twenty-two dollars soon after admission to the university. Students who lived on campus faced strict regulations. Rooms were open to inspection by the commander of cadets at any time.[56]

The curriculum for the Military Department was modeled after General Howard's training at West Point. Students were trained in infantry tactics, artillery tactics and special exercises. They were trained in the roles of soldiers, company and battalion. They also received weapons training. This meant they were taught the use of field guns and artillery, the sabre and bayonet. For physical education, or as it has been described "physical culture," gymnastics were included in the curriculum.[57]

With this establishment of the Military Department, Howard University essentially became a military academy. Students were awakened every morning between 5:00 and 6:00 a.m. with the sounds of reveille. Roll call was held every morning and night, with lights out at 10:30 p.m. Students were to march in companies to classes and meals. Study sessions were mandatory. Interaction with their superiors was regimented.[58]

Students were to behave in a prescribed manner in all interactions with faculty or members of the board of trustees. If passed by a member of either

The Main Building on the Howard University Campus. *Courtesy of the Howard University Archives.*

General Oliver Otis Howard. Howard was the head of the Freedmen's Bureau and the namesake of Howard University. Howard and his compatriots instilled a spirit of military service in the university that they founded. *Courtesy of the Howard University Archives.*

group, students were to stand and salute. If they were in the presence of a faculty member or trustee, the student was to stand at attention until told otherwise. This regimentation also extended to the students' dress as they lived with a strict dress code. Men were to wear pantaloons, vest, cap, buttons, bars and stripes at all times. Students were living "the life of a soldier."[59]

As in any military academy, rules were strictly enforced, and punishments were tough. For even small incidents, students were subject to arrest "within close or extended limits." If a student was caught smoking, chewing tobacco or playing cards, he was removed from university facilities. If a student was caught smoking or drinking alcohol, he would lose his scholarships. In fact, the use of tobacco or drinking alcohol made a student ineligible for financial assistance from the university. Living such regimented lives had a somewhat chilling effect on the student body.[60]

The campus of Howard University as it looked in 1870 at the start of the Military Department. *Courtesy of the Howard University Archives.*

C.S. Richards, principal of the Preparatory Department, described the effect of the students' regimented lives to the board of trustees. In the report, he stated: "They are sometimes improvident, excitable, self-confident and tenacious of their opinions yet on the whole they are docile, submissive and easily led by a firm and steady hand." It was clear that military training had the intended effect of creating good little soldiers.[61]

To the relief of many students, military instruction did not last long at the university. After three years, military instruction at Howard came to an end. On May 24, 1874, the board of trustees voted to abolish the Military Department. The Commercial Department also was abolished at this meeting. While no reason is given for the decision, an examination of the state of the university provides some insight. That same year, General Howard resigned as president of the university. Howard was, of course, the greatest supporter of the department at the university. At the time, the university found itself financially struggling. Indeed, the following year, the entire administration was made to resign and reapply for their jobs at half the pay. The closure of the Freedmen's Bureau in 1872 meant that the university could no longer rely on that institution for funding.[62]

With the end of the Military Department, Howard University's connection to the armed forces began to wane. At the same time, many of the ex-soldiers who founded the university were no longer in positions of power. The military spirit had dimmed at the university. Many of the students were happy to see the end of the militaristic environment. The department's closure, however, was not the end of military instruction at the university.

THE RETURN OF MILITARY INSTRUCTION TO HOWARD UNIVERSITY

At the beginning of World War I, Howard University restarted its military training programs. The campus itself had already been changed to resemble a war camp in support of the war effort. The administration was able to accomplish this thanks to an outbreak of influenza, which closed the school for regular instruction that year. Through the efforts of the student body, a training camp for African American officers was established in Des Moines, Iowa. Now it was Howard's turn to begin training men for war. While not officially departments of the university, these programs served as conduits for specialized army training for African American men. Their development led to a lasting program through which Howard would support the armed forces.

The first program established at the university during this period was the Student Army Training Camp (SATC). The program was authorized by the War Department Committee on Special Educational War Training at the behest of the administration and faculty from the university. The goal of the camp was to train military instructors so that they might begin programs at other schools. Led by Lieutenant Russell Smith, the SATC began in earnest on August 1, 1917, and 457 men from seventy colleges answered the initial call. Many of the men who participated in the SATC came to Howard with previous military training. Some came to the university from the Washington High School Cadet Corps.[63]

Under the provisions, camps were established at four locations around the country. The largest camp was Plattsburgh Barracks, New York, with 3,250 men. Camps were also established at Fort Sheridan, Illinois, and Presidio of San Francisco, California. The smallest camp was the camp established at Howard. Those who joined the camp were paid thirty dollars a month and expected to enlist for sixty days. After this term, they would be discharged from service.[64]

In training documents, it was made explicitly clear that during their period of training, the men "belong to the Army of the United States." As such, the program of instruction was extremely rigid. Training was set

and meant to cover four themes: discipline, precise, rigid and exacting. The most important aspect of this training was discipline. Since they belonged to the U.S. Army, the men were subject to military law. Having the proper discipline and decorum required was important for the men to reach the completion of the program.[65]

Although housed at Howard University, the SATC was open to students from other black colleges. This was, of course, a necessity, as it was the only camp for African Americans. Officers from other African American colleges were assigned to assist the Howard program. Officers from Fisk, Lincoln, Atlanta and Wilberforce Universities, as well as Hampton and Tuskegee Institutes, were assigned. In session for forty-five days, the first group completed instruction in September 1918. The SATC was demobilized on December 18, 1918, having trained 1,786 men. As a direct result of the program, twelve "A" or college-level units, fifteen vocational units and twenty informal military training units were established at twenty other schools. The camp was a success.[66]

In November 1917, the university established a radio school through the School of Manual Arts and Applied Sciences. The radio school was developed at the request of the Federal Board for Vocational Training, which wanted the university to assist in the training of African American men for the Signal Corps. In total, 135 men enrolled in the radio school. At the program's conclusion, three received first-class certificates, twenty received second-class certificates and the rest received third-class certificates. With their certificates in hand, the men were assigned to the 325th Field Signal Battalion at Chillicothe, Ohio.[67]

Howard University officers at the Reserve Officer Training Camp, Fort Des Moines, Iowa, July 22, 1917. *Courtesy of the Howard University Archives.*

African American Members of the U.S. Army Signal Corps at work in the jungles of the Pacific front. *Courtesy of the Manuscript Division, Moorland Spingarn Research Center.*

The Members of the Student Army Training Program at Howard University, 1917. *Courtesy of the Howard University Archives.*

The Army Specialized Training Program at Howard University

In 1943, Congress passed the Specialized Training Program Act. The act created training programs for engineers, doctors, dentists, language experts and other specialized fields. In support of this, the university began Company A, 2515th Service Unit Army Specialized Training Reserve Program. The men chosen for the program at Howard were picked for their academic prowess. All of the men had IQs of 120 or above.[68]

Students in the program received military scholarships from the federal government. The scholarships covered tuition, food and housing, clothing and healthcare. Participants were provided a full college curriculum. The course of study included training in mathematics, physics, chemistry, English, history, geography, physical education and military training. When looking at the enrollment numbers, the popularity of the program

Members of the Howard University Army Specialized Training Program, 1946. *Courtesy of the Howard University Archives.*

Lieutenant Wendell M. Lucas. Lucas was commissioned direct from the Reserve Corps in 1941 and awarded his wings from Aviation Cadet Corps at the Tuskegee Army Air Field. *Courtesy of the Howard University Archives.*

was evident. Students came to the program from twenty states and the District of Columbia.[69]

The ASTRP began training men for service in June 1943. Total enrollment for the program stood at 300. Most of the men were trained for medical and dental regiments. Unfortunately, the program lasted only a year. After graduation, 250 men were assigned to the Ninety-Second Infantry unit and spent much of their time in Italy. After the war, 60 of these men returned to Howard to finish their college education; however, only 41 graduated.[70]

The men trained at Howard University achieved great success while in the military and continued that success afterward. Members of the ASTRP and the Howard ROTC were part of the famed Tuskegee Airmen squadron. Other successful graduates include Luke C. Moore, who became the U.S. marshal for the District of Columbia. John Martin, a 1940 graduate of the Army ROTC, was appointed director of the D.C. Selective Service Board in 1946. Tuskegee Airman Wendell Lucas earned a BS in 1940, MS in 1942 and an MD in 1950 from Howard. He joined the faculty at the university in 1956. At the time of his death in May 1966, Lucas had become the chief of the division of urology at Howard.[71]

The ROTC at Howard University

World War I marked a turning point in the history of the university. Foremost, it restored the military spirit. During this period, the university made a number of curriculum changes to restore its support of a military program. This included hiring several instructors of military science. It also included making participation a requirement for graduation. In all, Howard University made a dedicated commitment to supporting the armed forces and military training after its experience during World War I. This led to the creation of the Reserve Officer Training Corps, which has become the life of the university's support of the armed forces.

The Reserve Officer Training Corps program at Howard University was said to have begun in the spring of 1918, shortly after the end of the officer training program established at the university to support World War I. The official announcement of the ROTC program at Howard was made on January 29, 1919. Interestingly, the official founding date of the organization is also sometimes given as February 13, 1919. The university's catalog for 1918–19 cites the February date. The program at Howard and one established at Wilberforce University are the first senior ROTC programs at historically black colleges. Following the establishment of these programs, junior ROTC units were established at other black schools, including Tuskegee Institute, Hampton Institute, North Carolina Agricultural & Technical University and Prairie View University.[72]

The first professor of military science hired under this new program was Captain Campbell C. Johnson. Johnson was assisted by First Lieutenant John Love. After Johnson left the program, Major Milton T. Dean was hired as professor of military science and tactics. Dean was assisted by Warrant Officer Edward York and Captain Julian DeCourt. This unit existed for several years until York was reassigned by the War Department in September 1921. This did not mean the unit was completely abandoned. The university retained DeCourt, and York (despite his reassignment) remained at the university to teach military science. The unit was reestablished in November of that same year.[73]

A group of seasoned military officers led the ROTC program during this period. The head of the program was Colonel Charles E.N. Howard, retired. Howard had considerable military knowledge. He graduated from the Coast Artillery School and served twenty-two months in France during World War I. Assistant professor of military science Major Joseph W. Blanchard served in the Spanish-American War and World War I. A graduate of Georgetown

Members of the first group of men to be commissioned through ROTC after the war began at the Charter Day banquet, 1946. *Courtesy of the Howard University Archives.*

University, Blanchard was known to be "forceful" but also a "big hearted friend" to the ROTC students.[74] Working with them were Captain Martin Rice, Sergeant Dorcey Rhodes, Sergeant Darwin Smith and Warrant Officer Roscoe E. Clayton.

The ROTC was given the use of Spaulding Hall for its activities. The program required the space not only for military training but also for its other roles on the campus. As mentioned earlier, nearly every male student at the university was required to participate in the program. With the mandate of providing physical activity for the student population, the ROTC was also responsible for the physical education program at the university. This meant that all students at the university were required to have some contact with the department.[75]

The curriculum developed for the ROTC program fell under the auspices of the Physical Education Department. Thirteen courses were developed as part of this program, with five dedicated to military science. The courses were described in the university catalogue:

> *PHYSICAL EDUCATION 10. Military Science. This course for the first and second years will include military courtesy and discipline; care and handling of arms and equipment; infantry drill regulations; small arms firing regulations; personal hygiene, first aid, and sanitation; interior guard duty; minor tactics; morale; military physical training; practical work in the liaison for different arms; topography and map reading; signaling.*

PHYSICAL EDUCATION 11. Military Science. This is a lecture course covering in the first and second years the scientific study of Infantry Drill Regulations; theory of target practice; military organization; map reading; personal hygiene; military history of the United States and military obligations of citizenship; service of information; and camp sanitation for small commands.

PHYSICAL EDUCATION 25. Military Science. This course for the third and fourth years will include, besides the subjects listed in Physical Education 10, the following: camp sanitation, baths and latrines, camp refuse, interior economy of company camps, sanitation and discipline, messes and water supply, minor tactics-combat of small units, small map problems, and tactical walks; field engineering tasks, and working parties; hasty entrenchments, obstacles, and material; law— civil and military; military policy.

PHYSICAL EDUCATION 26. Military Science. This is a lecture course covering, in the third and fourth years, studies in minor tactics; field orders; field engineering; map maneuvers; company administration; recent military history; elements of international law and military law; and details of property accountability.

PHYSICAL EDUCATION 27. Military Science. Construction of trenches, observation posts, camouflage, bridges, explosives and demolitions; cordage; company administration; military policy; military history; economics; military law—courts-martial; rules of land warfare; and hippology. For Seniors only.[76]

As a result of its rigorous curriculum, the program began to see immediate success. Students began receiving commissions soon after the start of the program. In February 1922, seventeen students were awarded commissions as second lieutenants by the War Department. The commissions were important not only as the first from the university but also as the first for African Americans from the War Department. They became a symbol of Howard advancing the cause of African Americans in the armed forces.[77]

As a reflection of the university's support of the ROTC program, 350 students were enrolled in the program by 1923. Supporting these numbers was the decision by the board of trustees to make military training compulsory. All physically fit male students were required to complete two years of military training. Without this training, they were not allowed to graduate. In 1923, the requirement was increased to three years. The curriculum was modified to reflect the same training provided by the War Department for senior infantry units. As mentioned previously, this course of study qualified students to receive commissions as second lieutenants. Between 1922 and 1942, 450 students received such commissions.[78]

An important component of the ROTC program at Howard was the ROTC band. Organized in 1920, the band was led by Sergeant Dorcey Rhodes. An important part of the university life, the band also contributed to the development of the Howard University Symphony Orchestra. The members of the ROTC band were also members of the orchestra, also led by Rhodes. The band performed at many local and national events, gaining prominence for precision and skill.[79]

Despite its successful integration into the curriculum of the university, the ROTC program was not without controversy during its early years. In 1925, the board of trustees voted to punish students who did not fully participate in the ROTC requirement. The board adopted a special rule stating that students who missed more than twenty of the daily ROTC or physical education courses would be expelled from the university. The student body was incensed and leapt into action in protest of the rule.[80]

Following the announcement of the "20-cut" rule, a group of students at the university began a strike on May 7, 1925. The students met at the Lincoln Theater on U Street to plan their response and drafted a letter to Howard president Stanley Durkee demanding an end to the rule and that

Commissioned second lieutenants from the ROTC at Howard University, circa 1920. *Courtesy of the Howard University Archives.*

HU ROTC Students at Fort Meade, Maryland, 1923. *Courtesy of the Manuscript Division, Moorland Spingarn Research Center.*

the compulsory education requirements be reduced to two years. With the intervention of the faculty, students returned to classes on May 14 under the threat of suspension. To settle the matter, students were allowed to return with no penalties and were only required to make up work missed. According to historian Rayford Logan, the "20-cut" rule was never enforced, and no students were expelled under the ruling.[81]

This marked a change in the Howard student population. As mentioned previously, the students were generally considered docile during the early years of the university. However, the 1920s marked a period of increased militancy among the African American population. This was caused by several factors. They included the effects of murders of black soldiers and race riots following the Red Summer of 1919 and the Harlem Renaissance. Led by Howard professor Alain Locke, the renaissance ushered in the era of the New Negro movement. Under this movement, African Americans would no longer accept their treatment as second-class citizens in the United States. Followers began agitating for and exercising their rights. Howard students were not immune to this movement.

Adding to the tense atmosphere surrounding the ROTC was the arrival of Howard's first black president, Mordecai Wyatt Johnson. Upon his arrival at the university, Johnson made significant changes to the administration of the university. While these changes caused much controversy, history has

The Howard University Orchestra, 1924. *Courtesy of the Howard University Archives.*

HU ROTC students participate in field exercises, circa 1920. *Courtesy of the Howard University Archives.*

shown that they moved the university toward its status as the "Capstone of Negro Education." Johnson was not a fan of activities he believed took the students' focus off education.

With this in mind, Johnson set out to dismantle sports, the ROTC and physical education programs at the university. In 1928, Johnson proposed that the administration abolish the ROTC program, but the proposal was defeated by a vote from the faculty. The faculty were more forward thinking on the issue of military education. They argued that the United States would fight wars in the future that would require black soldiers. Since there would be black soldiers, these men would need to be properly trained. It followed that Howard University as the capstone should be involved in this training. Eventually, Johnson came to this conclusion as well and dropped his desire to end the ROTC program.[82]

Despite the general rumblings regarding its relevance and attacks by the administration, the ROTC program persisted. By 1928, the results of the ROTC unit's hard work began to pay off. The program started receiving recognition from both the military and outside observers. During the summer of 1928, the unit participated in practical training at Camp Fort Leonard Wood. Over the six weeks of training, the group impressed all observers. At the end, the unit was rated third in general average for training and practice and first in administrative ratings. The group was also positively reviewed during the pass and review portion of President Herbert Hoover's inaugural parade.[83]

The entrenchment of the ROTC into the life of the university was further reflected by the creation of the Sabers. Organized on November 3, 1931, the Sabers was a club for officers in the ROTC with Lieutenant LeRoy A. Clay serving as its first president. The goals of the group were consistent with the general reasons that many African Americans gave for military service, to reflect their patriotism and earn their rights as citizens of the United States. The description of the organization stated: "The ideals of the SABERS are primarily, patriotism and citizenship. The organization promotes a wholesome respect for authority and encourages initiative and leadership. The Sabers stand for military courtesy, punctuality, truth and respect for self and others."[84]

During World War II, the ROTC program was expanded. In addition to other courses, the university added mandatory Red Cross first-aid instruction. The university also increased the number of credits allowed for ROTC from four credits to fifteen semester hours. This allowed for a larger enrollment in ROTC, which was the goal of the university. It wanted to stimulate the growth in African American officers. For its leadership's efforts,

ROTC instructors from the award-winning 1942 class. *Left to right*: Lieutenant Colonel Henry J. Boettcher, Captain Robert Wilson and Sergeant Earl Spreuill. *Courtesy of the Howard University Archives*.

ROTC members pose for group photograph, circa 1948. *Courtesy of the Howard University Archives*.

the ROTC program at Howard received the highest rating from the War Department in 1942.

As part of extracurricular activities, the ROTC sponsored a number of events. The most important was the annual ROTC military ball. At the event, the president of the university would recognize those cadets who practiced exemplary service. To help with this, the university elected its first "co-ed colonel" in 1947. The role of the co-ed colonel was to serve as a hostess at social functions and review the cadets on ROTC day. Jacqueline Frazier was elected by the cadets to be the first honorary co-ed colonel. During this period, women were not allowed to join the ROTC program. By introducing the co-ed colonel, the ROTC marked its first step toward allowing women to fully participate in the unit.

The program began to function normally after the demobilization of the specialized training programs created at the university during World War II. The first ROTC graduations since the end of World War II were held in 1949. The war's end saw several changes to the ROTC program at Howard managed by Frank Coleman. Coleman was credited with much of the continuing success of the ROTC. Under Coleman's leadership, the curriculum was updated to reflect the training programs of fifteen branches of the army. Prior to this period, the curriculum only reflected training for infantry divisions.[85]

The university began to celebrate the ROTC in earnest following the war as well. Part of this recognition came in the form of establishing ROTC Day. The day was administered by both the AFROTC and the Army ROTC. Marking the end of the ROTC program for the year, the day was filled with parades, a pass and review and several competitions between the cadets. President Mordecai Johnson and officials from the War Department were on hand to distribute awards and citations.[86]

War brought a considerable boost to the importance of ROTC programs at African American colleges, and Howard was no exception. Most of the support came from veterans. Their experiences in war highlighted the benefits of ROTC training. In particular, Korean War veterans from Howard promoted the value of the program. As soldiers, they learned that they had better experiences in the military as officers rather than entering as privates. Although Executive Order 9981 signed by President Harry Truman desegregated the military in 1950, the soldiers still understood that the treatment of black soldiers in the military varied greatly depending on one's status.[87]

Howard University's first honorary co-ed Cadet Colonel Jacqueline Frazier. Frazier was elected in a competition by the majority vote of men taking ROTC courses. *Courtesy of the Howard University Archives.*

In September 1947, the War Department created the U.S. Air Force as a separate branch of the military. In response, Howard created the Air Force ROTC Program, which meant the newly rebuilt ROTC program consisted of two separate units. Much like the Army ROTC, the Air Force ROTC program was an immediate success. In 1948, the AFROTC unit at Howard was named the best program in the nation in the area of air force supply. The competition included Ohio University, University of Florida and The Citadel. The program ranked no. 3 in the area of transportation training.[88]

An auxiliary organization to support the burgeoning ROTC program was soon created at the university. On December 11, 1950, the university installed the Andrew W. Turner Squadron of the Arnold Air Society. The group's first class consisted of sixteen cadets. Like the Sabers before it, the squadron was formed to foster a greater sense of purpose among its members. The purpose of the group was to encourage "greater teamwork, technical knowledge, and cooperation."[89]

Similar to the organization established in the air force program, the Army ROTC developed another organization to replace the Sabers. Scabbard and Blade was a national military honor society. Much like the Arnold Air Society, Scabbard and Blade sought to bring together various ROTC units from around the country. The end goal was to "foster and encourage the essential qualities of good and efficient officers." Clearly, the members of the ROTC understood the need for teamwork and the value it added to their studies.[90]

Company A. Army ROTC at Howard University, 1947. *Courtesy of the Howard University Archives.*

From left to right: Colonel James J. Carnes, Professor Frank Coleman, Lieutenant Colonel Harold Maull and Colonel Joseph T. Morris, 1948. *Courtesy of the Howard University Archives.*

Their respective drill teams were an important part of both programs. By the late 1960s, each team was nationally recognized for its talent. The Andrew D. Turner Air Force Drill Team won several competitions, including being named U.S. Western Champions. In 1968, the team also won the University of Maryland drill meet. The team took top honors in basic, trick and overall competition. The George F. Welch Army Drill team also took top honors in several competitions throughout the country. This included winning the Pratt Institute drill competition.[91]

In 1965, the university established women's auxiliaries for the ROTC programs. This was an extension of the honorary co-ed idea begun in the 1950s. To support the Army ROTC, the university created the "Armettes." The Armettes organized various community service events for the units. For the AFROTC program, the university created the "Aerodettes" as an auxiliary support unit in 1964. Not just a service organization, the Aerodettes also had a drill team. The team won many honors during its tenure.[92]

HU ROTC students pose for photograph in uniform, circa 1944. *Courtesy of the Howard University Archives.*

Another organization for women with an interest in supporting the air force was Angel Flight. Organized in November 1965, Angel Flight was created to support the men of the Arnold Air Society. In this capacity, the group functioned similarly to the Armettes. The group's description shared this three-part purpose: "To further the cause of the United States Air Force by promoting the interest of the college man in the AFROTC program, to aid in the progress of the men in the Arnold Air Society, and to serve as a symbol of appreciation for the importance and dignity of Air Force Life."

Angel Flight, like the other auxiliary organizations, managed community service events for the program. Part of a national organization, the group participated in conferences and service programs with other chapters. The program that provided the most pride to the group was its sponsoring of an orphan overseas.[93]

While still a popular field, ROTC faced challenges toward the end of the 1960s. As student unrest rocked the campus in the decade, the compulsory ROTC requirement was challenged. In fact, every year between 1962 and 1967, students protested the requirement. Anger over involvement in the Vietnam War combined with the burgeoning black power movement and students' rights movement on campus. The students' concerns over the requirement were twofold. The ROTC course requirement was a one-credit course. However, the amount of time required to successfully complete the course surpassed what was required for three-credit courses. Many students also felt that with the compulsory requirement, they were being "force fed [a] pill of military life."[94]

In April 1967, students disrupted an assembly by General Louis Hershey, head of the Selective Service board. The students (which included homecoming queen Robin Gregory) were disciplined by the university. This resulted in a protest by over four hundred students in which General Hershey, university president James Nabrit and College of Liberal Arts dean Frank Snowden were hung in effigy at the Delta tree. Hershey's effigy carried with it a sign reading "The best niggers are dead niggers" and was set ablaze. Nabrit and Snowden were referred to as "Uncle Tom." Students also expressed frustration with the war in Vietnam. Student Ronald Ross was quoted in the *Hilltop* student newspaper as saying that they were also protesting "the militarist, capitalist war 10,000 miles away."[95]

The question of compulsory ROTC was on the minds of many students during this period. Every edition of the *Hilltop* student newspaper carried articles, editorials and letters to the editor discussing the requirement. In one editorial, an anonymous student wrote in favor of the program. In the article, he stated that he supported ROTC for the useful information it provided to students, the discipline taught and the geography skills taught in the course. He also noted that the requirement was well known to students who applied to the university. The protesting students should just accept the requirement.[96]

In the spring of 1967, the Howard University Student Association (HUSA) put the idea of ending compulsory ROTC to a vote of the faculties of the various departments. The faculties of the College of Liberal Arts, School of Law, School of Social Work and School of Religion voted to support voluntary ROTC. The faculties of the College of Fine Arts, School of Engineering and Architecture and the Colleges of Dentistry and Medicine voted to keep compulsory ROTC. Those who voted to keep the program compulsory felt that the discipline provided by the program and the tradition of the requirement were most important.[97]

Students continued the protests of the compulsory ROTC requirement into the fall of 1967. Over 150 students walked out of the opening day exercises in Cramton Auditorium in September. The students were led by Ewart Brown, president of the student assembly; Barbara Penn, president of the Liberal Arts Student Council; and Tom Myles of the Student's Rights Organization. The members of the ROTC took the protests in stride. In response to the unrest, Major Pierre, acting professor of military science, stated: "I am in favor of anything that will better enable me to carry out my mission of providing qualified officers for the U.S. Armed Forces. We are presently achieving this goal. I cannot be sure the voluntary program will better aid me in achieving this goal because I have not witnessed such a program."[98]

A paper distributed to students after another student walkout in October explained students' feelings. The authors stated: "We the freshman class officers take the following position regarding compulsory ROTC: The institution of compulsory ROTC is not in keeping with the purpose of a university; compulsory ROTC violates the principles of academic freedom; compulsory ROTC denies personal liberties." Freshman class president Michael Harris found himself suspended after refusing to sign the oath of loyalty required for ROTC. He explained that the requirement to fight "domestic enemies" made him fearful. "I don't know who they are. It might one day mean black people, I don't know," stated Harris.[99]

The activity came to a head when protesters disrupted the freshman assembly, demanding an end to compulsory ROTC. During the program, students began to chant "no more ROTC." Following this disruption, the students led a sit-in at President Nabrit's office. Earlier in the day, the Ad Hoc Committee to Abolish Compulsory ROTC hung two dummies in effigy in front of Douglass Hall. After an emergency meeting of the board of trustees, the requirement was removed. The constant attack on the requirement of compulsory ROTC was a success. The result was a benefit for both the university and the student body.[100]

Left: ROTC Members being inspected during pass and review at Howard University. *Courtesy of the Howard University Archives*.

Below: Major Rayford instructs students in the advanced ROTC class, 1946. *Courtesy of the Howard University Archives*.

To maintain the relevance of the program, the Army ROTC updated the curriculum again to make it more relevant to the student population and support the community. These changes were made under the leadership of Lieutenant Colonel Maurice Williams, who joined the university in September 1969. These changes included the addition of courses in revolution and theories and guerilla warfare, and military history was updated to include the contributions of African Americans to the military. The group also extended its community service efforts. The Army ROTC began a mentoring and tutoring program for preteens at the N.W. Settlement House. The goal of the program was to teach leadership and teamwork.[101]

The AFROTC program also changed its program to remain in step with the USAF Air Commandos. It included courses in warfare, counterinsurgency tactics and procedures. The update in training paid off for the program when it participated in national competitions. In 1970, Cadet Lieutenant Colonel Richard Evans beat out over two hundred competitors to win the Vice Commandant Award during summer camp training at Pease Air Force Base in New Hampshire.[102]

The 1970s also saw a big change in the ROTC programs at Howard. For the first time, women were allowed to join the ROTC. Linda M. Miles was the first woman to join the AFROTC program. The next year, she was joined by Judy Atkinson and Nina Harper. By 1975, there were also women in the Army ROTC program.

Another significant change to the ROTC program came during this period. Although based at Howard, the AFROTC saw its makeup begin to include many students from schools throughout the District of Columbia. By 1982, 45 percent of the students in the AFROTC were from schools other than Howard. As students continued to join the ROTC for reasons including patriotism, parental influence and financial aid, the numbers of students throughout the district continued to increase. Today, the makeup of the unit is about 50 percent Howard students and 50 percent students from the district.

The ROTC programs at Howard have produced an impressive roster of military professionals. They include: General Lester Lyles of the U.S. Air Force, Major General Robert C. Gaskill, Major General Alvin Bryant, Major General Cunningham C. Bryant, Major General John R. Hawkins III, Major General George A. Alexander, Major General Andrew W. Chambers, Major General Michael Harrison, Brigadier General Guthrie L. Turner, Brigadier General Robert A. Harelston, Brigadier General Vernon C. Spaulding Jr. and Brigadier General Melvin L. Byrd of the army. Notably,

Howard alumnus the Honorable Togo D. West Jr. was appointed secretary of the army by President Bill Clinton.

The ROTC at Howard University has seen many changes throughout the years. Its beginning as a compulsory program for all physically fit male students saw it become one of the largest operations on the campus. With the arrival of World War II and subsequent wars, the program has seen its fortunes at the university rise and fall. While not as prominently featured as in years past, both the Army and Air Force ROTC programs have had a significant impact on the university. Both programs are nationally recognized for their excellence in training. Performing in the service of democracy is still a part of the activity at Howard University.

THE HOWARD UNIVERSITY
MEN AND WOMEN IN THE
ARMED FORCES TELL THEIR STORIES

The story of African Americans in World War II has been told many places. There are many written tales of the battles and stories of the heroism of African American soldiers. Included in those documents are also stories of the racism faced by those soldiers during their tenure. None of those stories is more powerful than the ones told by the soldiers themselves. They include tales of despair as well as tales of hope for the future and what the world could become. The stories told by soldiers from Howard University cover the gamut of the African American experience in the war.

During the war, Howard University faculty and staff developed ways to support their alumni fighting overseas. One of the first actions was to form a committee focused solely on supporting the troops. Major figures in the project included Howard president Mordecai Wyatt Johnson, Secretary James Nabrit, Professor Merze Tate and Moorland Collection librarian Dorothy Porter Wesley. The group maintained regular correspondence with those alumni they could find. They also sent care packages to the soldiers in an effort to boost morale.

For her part, Dorothy Porter Wesley sought to document the stories of these men and women in the Moorland Collection. The letters were gathered by request from the committee or given to Porter by professors who themselves remained in contact with former students. Each letter expressed love of the institution and offered insight into personal experiences while serving at home or abroad. Letters were received from nearly every front describing duties, activities and thoughts.

Dorothy Porter in the library at Howard University. Porter was the major figure in preserving the letters of the Howard Men and Women in the Armed Forces. *Courtesy of the Manuscript Division, Moorland Spingarn Research Center.*

HOWARDITES IN THE WAR

The majority of the letters received by the university from the alumni serving in the armed forces covered general observations about military service and the areas in which their authors' served. Captain George C. Marshall recounted that his experience in the armed forces was a "paradox." Captain Marshall spent his time traveling from Europe to Northern Africa. In the Azores Islands, he observed that an Allied air field and a German air field sat one mile apart from each other. The fields were only separated by a small rise. Marshall noted that the two sides generally ignored each other—although some members claimed that the two spied on one another. Marshall also noted his disdain for Casablanca. He commented that it was not a beautiful city like he imagined but was "filthy." This disdain extended to the people. Besides being dirty, he also said the city was "teeming with all manner of human debris." He was, however, impressed with Cairo, Egypt.

Ahnestacia Scott, personnel service director of the American Red Cross, 1943. *Courtesy of the Howard University Archives.*

In his estimation, Cairo was the "most beautiful city," and he enjoyed the people. He reserved his greatest praise for a sight he saw in India. One evening, he and his crew observed the Taj Mahal lit by moonlight. To him, this was "the most beautiful and spectacular sight of the whole trip."[103]

In her letter to Howard, Ahnestacia E. Scott described her observations as it related to race and ethnicity in the United Kingdom. Scott's work with the American Red Cross allowed her to interact with many different groups. During her tour of duty, she traveled through several different cities, including London, Liverpool, Bristol, Salisbury, Leicester, Cheltenham, Torquay, Oxford, Stratford-on-Avon and Cardiff. One of her first observations was the difference between the black population in Great Britain and that in the United States. While she did not describe the differences in detail, she noted that they were caused by variances in the treatment each group received. She did, however, note that she was impressed with the kindness of the black population in England.[104]

Another of her observations falls in line with what many black servicemen and women experienced during their time in World War I.

Many African Americans who served had little experience with people of other cultures. Scott noted that traveling with the military changed her worldview for the better. For the soldiers, it did much to remove the negative opinion of others created by what she described as the "insidious propaganda" spread about other cultures. After spending time with friendly foreign populations, many of the soldiers found themselves impressed with the people and their lifestyles. However, Scott did note that it made her appreciate the United States more. "One is quite unable to fully appreciate the ideals of a democracy until one sees at first hand the undemocratic form of government."[105]

Letters like the ones from Henry Sideboard reflected the soldier's keen interest in events happening at home and how they could affect morale. The packages of black magazines and newspapers did much to help the morale of his fellow soldiers in New Guinea. Reflecting this interest, Sideboard requested copies of popular African American publications the *Afro Weekly*, *Pittsburgh Courier*, *Chicago Defender* and *Howard University Bulletin*. They were particularly interested in the publication *Strange Fruit* by Lillian Smith. Many of the soldiers felt that the publication truly captured their experiences back home in the South. Many hoped that publications such as this would help to improve race relations back in the United States.[106]

In his letter, Sideboard noted that many of the soldiers were devastated by the death of President Franklin Roosevelt. They took the death personally, and it greatly affected morale. For many, Roosevelt and his wife, Eleanor, were true champions for the black race. "Frankly, I believe we as a race achieved more under his administration than we have ever achieved before," said Sideboard.[107]

The weather was a challenge for many soldiers in general. Henry Sideboard remarked in his letter to librarian Dorothy B. Porter that he struggled with the weather in the Philippines. "The weather here in the Philippines is almost unbearable. For a full year and a half I've had a continuous, never-ending summer. The first winter back in the states will probably be the end of me."[108]

Some letters detailed major battles from the war. In his letter to Howard, John Marshall gave a detailed description of the Battle of Normandy. Marshall was working with the Seventy-Ninth Division as it stormed Utah Beach in France and forced a German retreat. The division marched over 180 miles and used "10 tons of ammunition" to forcefully defeat the Germans. Due to censorship and the need for secrecy, letters such as this were extremely rare.[109]

While many soldiers lamented their experience in the military, some had joyful experiences and even missed the military when they left. One such person was Eva Mae Williams. Williams worked as an American Red Cross "clubmobile" worker. After she returned home on an emergency furlough, the Red Cross released a press release detailing Williams's desire to return to Noyon, France. Williams was quoted in the press release: "I'd give anything to go back to my GI's." Whenever she and her group would arrive at the various camps, the men would yell, "Come on men! Here are the doughnut girls!" They would also engage in banter. While they had a joyful time, the women were still in danger. As they made the thirty-mile daily trek, the women often dodged attacks by "robot bomb." They also worked under less than good conditions. Their camp had no running water or other conveniences. Despite this, they persevered, using the motto "C'est la guerre!" or "There's a war on." Lifting the spirits of the soldiers was Williams's greatest benefit.[110]

Black nurses somewhere in England. Many black nurses served with pride and the knowledge that they playing a major role in supporting the war effort. *Courtesy of the National Archives and Records Administration.*

Left: Geneva Holmes served with the American Red Cross during World War II. *Courtesy of the Howard University Archives.*

Right: Julia Lilmarth Johnson. Johnson worked with the American Red Cross in England, 1945. *Courtesy of the Howard University Archives.*

Like Eva Williams, Geneva Holmes also shared positive experiences working with the servicemen through the Red Cross. Holmes, who spent over four years overseas, detailed her time working for the American Red Cross Duchess Street Service Club. According to Holmes, the Red Cross was extremely generous in providing funds to support the club. This effort was appreciated by the soldiers. She explained that the clubs provided a popular area of relief for many soldiers.[111]

Some of the soldiers had a very enjoyable time serving in the armed forces. This perspective was also reflected in the letters from GIs sent back to the university. A good example of this was the letter written by Rollin Williams. During his stay at Camp Clipper, California, he regularly traveled to Los Angeles on weekends. While there, Williams attended Hollywood parties with Bing Crosby, Bob Hope and Lena Horne. He was particularly excited that he had the experience of sitting next to Horne at a party. According to Williams, the Hollywood community was very supportive of servicemen when they encountered the stars. He also went horseback riding along the Pacific. His only complaint about being in the military was the heat. He

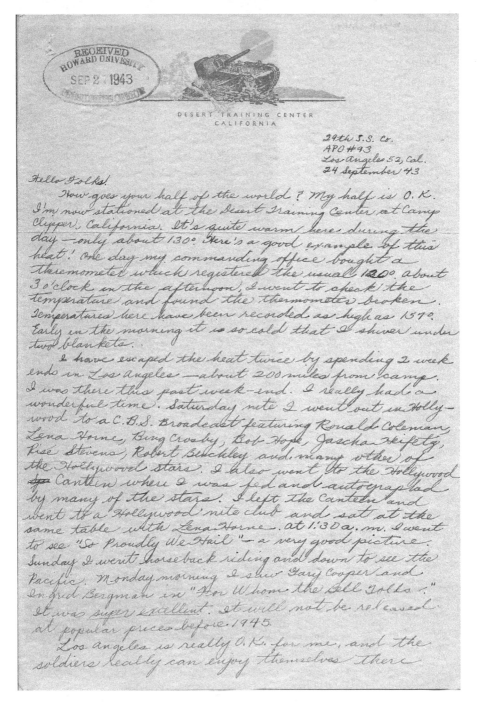

RECEIVED
HOWARD UNIVERSITY
SEP 2 1943

DESERT TRAINING CENTER
CALIFORNIA

24th S.S. Co.
APO #93
Los Angeles 52, Cal.
24 September '43

Hello Folks!

How goes your half of the world? My half is O.K. I'm now stationed at the Desert Training Center at Camp Clipper, California. It's quite warm here during the day — only about 130°. Here's a good example of this heat! One day my commanding office bought a thermometer which registered the usual 120°. About 3 o'clock in the afternoon, I went to check the temperature and found the thermometer broken. Temperatures here have been recorded as high as 157°. Early in the morning it is so cold that I shiver under two blankets.

I have escaped the heat twice by spending 2 week ends in Los Angeles — about 200 miles from camp. I was there this past week-end. I really had a wonderful time. Saturday nite I went out in Hollywood to a C.B.S. Broadcast featuring Ronald Coleman, Lena Horne, Bing Crosby, Bob Hope, Jascha Heifetz, Rise Stevens, Robert Benchley and many other of the Hollywood stars. I also went to the Hollywood Canteen where I was fed and autographed by many of the stars. I left the Canteen and went to a Hollywood nite club and sat at the same table with Lena Horne. At 1:30 a.m. I went to see "So Proudly We Hail" — a very good picture. Sunday I went horseback riding and down to see the Pacific. Monday morning I saw Gary Cooper and Ingrid Bergman in "For Whom the Bell Tolls." It was super excellent. It will not be released at popular prices before 1945.

Los Angeles is really O.K. for me, and the soldiers really can enjoy themselves there

Letter from Rollin C. Williams to Howard University. *Courtesy of the Manuscript Division, Moorland Spingarn Research Center.*

mentioned in his letter that on some days the temperature would reach as high as 157 degrees. During his brief stay at Fort Huachuca, he attended bullfights in Mexico.[112]

One of the more interesting stories contained in the letters is the account of Chaplain Darneal F. Johnson. Johnson was a 1932 graduate of the Howard School of Divinity and assistant pastor of the Metropolitan Baptist Church in Washington, D.C. While in the service, he recounted that he had to be resourceful. This included holding church services in the mess hall and on boats.[113] Dozens of Howard alumni served as chaplains throughout the armed forces. While makeshift, many of these services served to maintain the morale of the soldiers.

Music and entertainment were important in maintaining morale. Henry Sideboard noted that his division created a glee club. In his letter to Howard, Sideboard asked if the School of Music could send them musical arrangements they could perform. He was very specific in his request.

Entertainment was an important part of maintaining morale among the soldiers. In this photograph, members of the U.S. Army Signal Corps head to an on-base event. *Courtesy of the Manuscript Division, Moorland Spingarn Research Center.*

Dorothy Donegan with soldiers during a break in wartime action. Entertainment was particularly important to the morale of soldiers on the front lines. *Courtesy of the Manuscript Division, Moorland Spingarn Research Center.*

Sideboard explained he only wanted songs "arranged in <u>four parts</u> for <u>men's</u> voices," his emphasis.[114] However, even with the support of Howard, morale was hard to maintain for African American soldiers in the face of their realities.

George Leighton expressed many of his observations about the work of black soldiers and how this work was viewed. He shared these thoughts in a series of letters sent to Howard. Leighton reflected on the work conducted by African American soldiers and how it was viewed by the outside world. He observed that despite their sometimes ill treatment, black soldiers performed their duties with pride and success:

> *I have seen Negro engineers building roads over which important supplies have gone from depot to ships. I have seen Negro quartermaster battalions organize and operate depots that supplied frontline troop in contact with the*

enemy thousands of miles away. I have seen ordnance companies composed
of colored troops handling vital ammunition supply. Then, I have seen
Negro combat troops doing their share.

Leighton did lament the coverage that this work received in the press. He felt the reports were highly inaccurate. He also felt that they were an embarrassment to the black soldiers; in his mind, they mischaracterized the work of black soldiers. He saved much venom for the coverage provided by black newspapers, which he accused of publishing "pitifully asinine reports" on the activities of black soldiers.[115]

He noted that while the white press often ignored the success of black soldiers, the African American press exaggerated. Black newspapers often printed flattering stories of black soldiers gallantly fighting. While this did happen, as Leighton correctly pointed out, much of the work of black soldiers was in the area of "service and supplies." As discussed earlier, this owes much to do with the discriminatory attitudes about the aptitude of black soldiers in combat situations. These ideas led to the group being relegated to service positions.[116]

THOUGHTS ON RACE AND RACISM

Outside of the dangers of war, race was a large factor in whether black soldiers had a positive or negative experience while in the military. As we saw earlier, many soldiers enjoyed their experiences in the military. However, the specter of race was ever present throughout their lives. Many of the letters sent to Howard reflected this precarious existence.

One of the letters that captured the feeling of many of the soldiers heading to war was one written by John Lovell Jr. In a December 1943 letter to President Mordecai Johnson, Lovell recounted a disturbing scene on the bus to Camp Lee in Virginia. While riding, he noticed the faces of the other men riding with him. Their faces reflected a "hollowness of wondering if anyone really cared for their personal, <u>particular</u> discomfiture and sacrifice." For many black soldiers, the idea of fighting for their country made them proud. However, the reality of the intense racism they faced at home always tainted the joy and pride they felt for serving their country.[117]

Robert McDaniel articulated many of the frustrations felt by black soldiers throughout the armed forces. He shared that despite their difficulties, the soldiers were representing Howard well. He wrote:

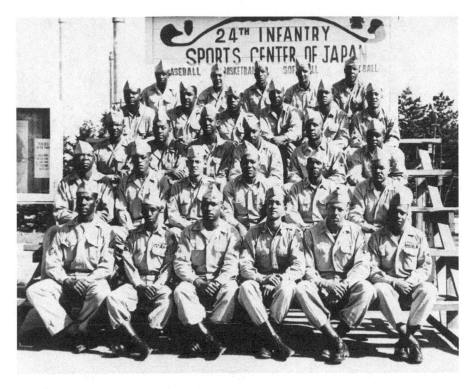

This is an image of the African American soldiers in the Twenty-Fourth Infantry Division in Japan. Many Howardites served in this division and throughout the Pacific front. *Courtesy of the Manuscript Division, Moorland Spingarn Research Center.*

There are quite a few alumni of Howard serving over here in the South Pacific. All are doing [a] fine job upholding the traditions and reflecting the training we received there, despite extremely unpleasant conditions. Besides the usual factors that place great strain on men at the front during war, the colored officers here have a very bitter and insidious presences put on them by prejudice and discrimination.... [B]ecause of a lack of rank, they are powerless to improve the condition to any extent. As a [illegible] they get an express of dangerous assignments and missions and of course receive no promotions above 1st Lieut. in the line regardless of merit.[118]

In a letter to Howard, George Leighton shared his observations about how race affected black soldiers. Leighton was particularly shaken by the racism he witnessed while in military service. He remarked in his letter that the experiences he faced and witnessed made him lose his faith in military service.

Mabel K. Staupers (*center*) and other World War II nurses salute while posing for a photograph. Staupers led the effort to integrate the U.S. Army Nursing Corps. *Courtesy of the Manuscript Division, Moorland Spingarn Research Center.*

He also shared that it even shook his faith in the future for African Americans in the United States. He shared that many of his fellow soldiers were suffering from depression as a result of their treatment. The effect of racism was also seen in their development as soldiers. Racism often led the soldiers to be ill-equipped for their current positions and unqualified to move to others.[119]

In Karachi, India, George Marshall observed racism in the competition for the attention of local women amongst the soldiers. He noted that many white soldiers were caught disparaging black soldiers to the local women. Often they would tell the women that the black soldiers had tails and were rapists. They also referred to them as "coalies," a racist term referring to their dark skin color. As he observed, this agitation eventually reached a boiling point and led to brawls among the soldiers.[120]

Not every African American in the service experienced racism while on active duty. One such letter came to Howard from an alum who identified himself as "Sergeant Lundy," who reported that he did not experience any racism while in the service. He was particularly impressed with his treatment and the actions of his superiors, who ensured that open racism was not tolerated in the "transportation corps." According to Lundy, "Colonel Ackerman would not hesitate to wash a man out who openly spoke the word 'nigger.'"[121]

Lieutenant Lucia A. Pley shared that the discrimination she faced did not come from the military but from the people in the town where she was stationed. Pley was one of a handful of black service members working at Station Hospital in Arizona. Despite this, she expressed that she received the respect due an officer from the white soldiers and German prisoners of war. The discrimination came when they had to leave the base and travel throughout Florence. She wrote, "We regret very much that the discrimination in the town around here is awful. We pray that soon we can walk into any restaurant, or soda fountain and be served food and drink. And to think any of these P.W.s can go any place and be served. On this part they get the best of everything." This experience was repeated at other installations both at home and abroad.[122]

Race and racism colored the experiences of African Americans both abroad and at home during the world war era. Serving their country through the armed forces added another element. Many African Americans felt pride that they were serving their country. Like in previous wars, many believed that their hard work and dedication would go far toward ending racism at home. However, many discovered that racism simply followed them into the service. The indignities they experienced at home followed them abroad. However, this experience did not dampen many of their hopes for the future.

THE HU MEN AND WOMEN IN THE ARMED FORCES LOOK TOWARD THE FUTURE

During times of war, soldiers often have little time to reflect on their current situations, much less look toward the future. However, many of the HU men and women in the armed forces shared their desires and thoughts about the future. Some wanted to improve their education. Others hoped for a world of peace and no more wars. All of them had high hopes for what the future would hold.

Sometimes, the realities of war made soldiers think dark thoughts, but they maintained a hope for the future. In his letter to Howard, Harry McBeth noted his fears and concerns about the future of the African American race and the world in general. He noted his joy at receiving the newsletters sent by Howard to its students in the military but noted his sadness of reading about those who lost their lives in battle. He said, "How I do hope that clouds of death, hatred and devastation will soon go away. Then we all can look and behold the radiant light of peace on Earth and good will to Men."[123]

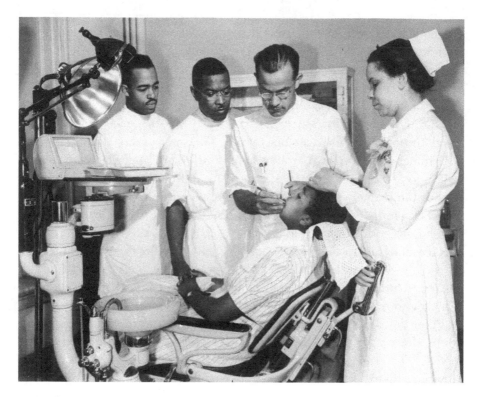

Howard University ASTP dental students, including Harry Mclinn and Dr. John H. Turner. *Courtesy of the Howard University Archives.*

In a letter dated August 30, 1944, Howardite Frederic Clanagan shared with excitement the reaction of the French people to the success of the Allies. Speaking of his time following the liberation of Paris, he shared:

> *The minute you dismount from your vehicle you are kissed and hugged and mauled by frenzied, friendly, elated mobs until you are left speechless; even though you do know a little French, you are left speechless, "merci" being the most overworked French word. You just say that. The gatherings are represented by little children and old women, grown up men and beautiful French girls! Most of them have bright flags of various sizes both British, American (with yet thirteen stars), and the tri-color.*

Despite the joy he felt from this reaction, his joy was sobered upon thinking about his return to the United States. He lamented having to return to the United States to fight racism and hatred. "Helping others to see the light again is quite alright and in actuality there is so much of the same thing which we fight remaining across the Atlantic—at home untouched in a sense." In a letter dated October 16, 1944, Clanagan seemed more upbeat about the prospects of race relations after the war. He stated that he believed that the war would improve "race unity" internationally.[124]

Clanagan also spent his time thinking about how the soldiers serving overseas would be reintegrated into society:

> *I have been more or less trying to visualize the average "GI" his reactions after the war; what he will be thinking, how he will utilize his discovered abilities and experiences. No doubt the civilian population back in America can best judge that now and make a pretty accurate account. It has been pointed out very clearly that the record of education in America is far below for being that only 23.3% of troops in the armed forces finished four years of high school, another 3.6% had four years or more of college, totaling 70% of the American men of fighting age have had less than a high school education. There will be a great influx to the many colleges and universities. In time of peace there was but very little money appropriated for education in comparison to war time conversions, yet in less than three years we can throw, equip, handle and feed 10,000,000 men to master the weapons of war to kill with no cry of "too much money." Billions of dollars poured in and many more needed before the final victory. While a few thousand a year formally spent for teaching peace to avoid war.[125]*

Howardite Edgar Davis shared his concerns over the future but explained that during his time in the service, he developed a plan for his postwar life. Upon completion of his tour of duty, Davis planned to become a junior accountant. Davis also developed a plan for the university as well. He shared this plan in a letter dated May 30, 1944:

> *Here's the idea. An Advisory Bureau staffed with qualified personnel from each department composed of professors and top ranking students would be able to state job possibilities in their respective fields. Facts could be gathered from such sources as the Library of Congress, governmental agencies and other organizations. This information could be complied and published or held ready for distribution for any interested persons.*

He included that he knew this would be a hit with returning service members and the Howard community at large. Interestingly, the university has created an office similar to what Davis recommended.[126]

Many soldiers like Lovell sought ways to extend the equality they felt in the military to civilian life. While he spoke of the despondence he witnessed in the faces of many African American soldiers as they headed out to war, John Lovell also spoke of a hope for the future. In his letter, he noted that being the armed forces and fighting for their lives forced men to forget their prejudices and come together. It was Lovell's hope that someone would find a way to develop a program to bring people together without war.[127]

Rollin Williams also expressed his thoughts of the future in his letters to the university. As we saw earlier, Williams did not spend much of his time abroad. Much of his time was spent training and providing support at home. This did not stop him from hoping for an end to the war and a better world to follow. In his letter, he expressed the hope that "the world will live in peace and tranquility and all men and nations shall better understand each other."[128]

Many of the soldiers were excited about the "veterans education program" established at Howard for returning soldiers. J.E. Raynor, who like many other servicemen spent time at Fort Huachuca in Arizona, expressed his desire to return to campus after the war was over so that he could participate in the program. Expressing his delight, he ended the letter with "Long live Howard University, all its administrative officers, Deans and Faculty! May all the Sons of Howard be ever bold to battle wrong."[129] Thinking of Howard was a major part of the Howardites' lives as they spent time abroad.

The Love of Dear Ol' Alma Mater

A love of Howard and an admiration for the support the soldiers received is evident in much of the correspondence sent to the university. James Keaton wrote to the university to update his address but also included a statement of love for the university. Keaton said, "I gladly express my gratitude relative to the bulletin received. The university is a credit to mankind and may it continue its advancements."[130] This spirit was reflected in nearly all of the letters sent to the university from its alumni fighting abroad and serving at home.

Frederick Wilkinson (Buddy)
Washington, D. C.

Commerce

Howard Players: Commerce Club. Pres.; Kappa Mu; R.O.T.C. Major; Achievement Key.

Augustine Williams
Washington, D. C.

Choir, Women's League.

Joshua Sloan Williams, Jr. (Josh)
Macon, Georgia

Zoology

Freshman Class Officer; American Student Union; Omega Psi Phi Fraternity; Tutor, Men's Dormitory Tutorial Staff.

Madlyn Williams
Washington, D. C.

English

Delta Sigma Theta Sorority; Historical Society; Women's League; Wesley Foundation; Classic Club; Ballet Club.

Marian Williams
St. Louis, Kentucky

Home Economics

Glee Club.

Robert M. Williams (Bob)
Atlanta, Georgia

Zoology

Football, end; Basketball; Glee Club; Wesley Foundation, Sec.; Omega Psi Phi.

William S. Willis
Texas

Philosophy and History

Dean's Honor Roll.

Margaret Wilburn (Bumps)
Asheville, North Carolina

Sociology

Women's League

Ernest J. Wilson
Philadelphia, Pennsylvania

Zoology

Student Council; Fellowship Council; German Club; Glee Club, Pres.; Tutor; Omega Psi Phi; Soccer; Howard Players; Delta Phi Delta; Achievement Key; Stylus.

Ann Young

Frederick Wilkinson was one of many Howardites to serve in the military. *Courtesy of the Howard University Archives.*

John C. Robinson of the class of 1940 was one soldier who noted with jubilation his exploits in reply to the request from the committee on the Howard Men and Women in the Armed Forces. He noted that the Ninety-Third Division, of which he was a part, completed three campaigns against the Japanese military. He did note with disappointment that their operations did keep Howardites from having much time to chat with one another and "chew the fat."[131] Although they did not know each other previously, a connection to Howard was usually enough to build a friendship.

George Snipes of the 1697th Engineer Combat Battalion included in his correspondence how excited he was to have Howardites as a part of his battalion. Snipes's commanding officer was Captain Beatric F.R. Lawson D.C., a 1942 graduate of Howard, and First Lieutenant William Atkinson, a 1938 graduate, was the battalion's dental surgeon.[132] Having someone with a connection back home provided solace for many of the men and women

Tuskegee Aviators reviewing war plans. Many Howardites were among the famed Tuskegee Airmen squadron. The squadron is one of the most accomplished African American units in the U.S. military. *Courtesy of the Manuscript Division, Moorland Spingarn Research Center.*

Letter from Frederic Clanagan to Howard University. *Courtesy of the Manuscript Division, Moorland Spingarn Research Center.*

in the armed forces. Many spent years overseas away from their families, and any connection to home became extremely important.

Those serving on the homefront also felt joy at seeing other soldiers with whom they shared a connection. George Walker found excitement in having fellow Howardites in his battalion. There were eight Howard soldiers serving with him and eight others in various units throughout Aberdeen Proving Ground in Maryland.[133] For Walker, this meant that he would have others to sit with, share experiences and reminisce.

Frederic Clanagan noted in his letter that he made sure to keep up with the progress of his fellow Howardites through the newspapers and correspondence sent to the front by the Howard faculty and staff. He was impressed that many of the soldiers found time to get married while serving.[134] In another letter, he expressed his love and excitement for the support that Howard provided him. "I am ever reminded of that good old genuine 'Howard Spirit,' deep down in my heart a flame was a glow on the recession just as the electric ones [candles] burned in your window."

The excitement of being included in the directory of Howard service members and receiving publications from Howard was, of course, not shared by those who discovered that they were missed. In a letter from North Burma, Marvin Fisk noted that he knew pain, grief and suffering, "Many of us know grief, know what it means to be in severe pain, and withstanding human torture and also the tortures of nature." But he noted that no one would know of their experience or that they existed because they were not included in the directory or the Howard bulletin. Despite this omission, he closed with "I want you to know we think of Howard and love her very much. Regards to all Howardites."[135]

Some soldiers were surprised by the types of Howard men they would meet. Thomas Luck had the benefit of meeting Major Hugh Simmons at the 268th Station Hospital. Luck enjoyed his encounter, referring to Simmons as "quite an interesting character." Maintaining a connection to the university was helpful to Luck as he spent his time in the army. Upon receiving the *Howard Bulletin* dedicated to the armed forces, he remarked: "It is quite gratifying to realize that in spite of one's remoteness from a civilized world; there are still some friends who consider you."[136]

A love of home and a thankfulness for the support they received from Howard was a running theme throughout the letters sent back to Howard.

A GIFT FROM HOME

The faculty and staff of the university did much to let the service members know that they were not forgotten. This is why the university made sure to send gift packages to the service members. The soldiers were excited to receive the gifts. This love was reflected in the letters sent back to Howard.

Many of the soldiers who received the gift packages of books and newspapers from Howard were excited to receive the gift. In numerous letters received by the university, the soldiers remarked on the helpfulness of the material when there was a break in fighting. In his letter to the university, Thaddeus Hobbs noted that when he opened his package, another soldier immediately took on the *Negro Digest*s. Upon receiving a second package, Hobbs shared that the books did much to improve morale among the soldiers, and they appreciated being able to keep up to date on events back home.[137]

Similar to Hobbs, Private First Class Thomas Luck was excited to receive the care package as well. He noted that before receiving the package, he was losing morale and inspiration. Luck was suffering from a sense of "stagnation." While he was constantly moving, in the military he felt the progression of his life had stagnated. He did take some solace in the notion that he was fighting to protect the life he wanted to live. He understood that he could only live the life he wanted if we lived in a world of freedom and peace.[138]

Wendell Lucas wrote a colorful letter describing his desire to receive a copy of the *Howard Bulletin*. Upon learning that others received a copy of the bulletin and he did not, Lucas wrote what must be considered a tongue-in-cheek note to Secretary Nabrit. In the letter, recipients were asked to close their eyes and think back to their time at Howard. He remarked that he could not do so and continue to read the letter. He also remarked on the changes he heard happening on the campus:

> *I observe that the university is struggling through an extremely crucial period in its history. Women running a student council and the* Hilltop*!! I wouldn't be surprised that they are presiding over the classes too. Next thing you know they'll be flying airplanes, voting, and drilling with the A.S.T.P. Good luck to them. I'm sure they're doing the good job (considering their innate handicaps).*

Considering the tone of the overall letter, it is safe to also assume that Lucas was being facetious with this provocative statement as well.[139]

Above, left: Frank Lucius Colbert, U.S. Navy, graduated from basic indoctrination as honor man of his company at the U.S. Naval Training Center, Great Lakes, Illinois. Colbert was elected candidate by fellow African American bluejackets and selected honor man by his company commander on the basis of military aptitude and progress. *Courtesy of the Howard University Archives.*

Above, right: Flight Officer Thurston L. Gaines. Gaines was commissioned from the Aviation Cadet Corps at the Tuskegee Army Air Field. *Courtesy of the Howard University Archives.*

Left: One of many Howard women to support the war effort, Viola B. Murphy was sent to England to serve the armed forces as an American Red Cross staff assistant, 1945. *Courtesy of the Howard University Archives.*

John Powell was another Howardite excited to receive a gift package from the university. He noted that the package did much to lift the morale of the soldiers. He promised to continue communication with the committee but made sure to let them know that he could only share information if it was permissible by the military.[140] Similarly, John Quick expressed his thanks for receiving a package. Quick received regular communications from the university and expressed his thanks. A pilot, Quick was trained at the Hondo Army Air Field and took a bombarding course at the SAAAF Bombardier School in San Angelo, Texas. After his training he became a bombardier-navigator with the 477th Bomber Group.

In a letter from a Howard alumnus simply signed "Jerry," the author expressed how grateful he was for the care packages and how much it helped him while witnessing the atrocities of war. Writing from the Italian front, "Jerry" shared: "My observations of the brutal realities of war have been heart rending. We can but trust that those in whose hands our destiny lies will deliver us to better days. Thank you again for making life in combat more bearable."[141]

IN THEIR OWN WORDS

The HU men and women in the armed forces were at the front lines of the battle against the spread of fascism during World War II. Many have told their stories, but hearing from the soldiers themselves provides a deeper understanding of their experiences. The sense of pride and hope for the future expressed in the following letters tell the story of how even in war, hope remains. Boosting the morale of these men and women was an important service provided by the university.

LETTERS FROM HOWARD MEN AND WOMEN IN THE ARMED FORCES

A note on the letters from Howard men and women in the armed forces: During World War II, the Howard University community responded with enthusiasm. Much like African Americans had done since the American Revolution, these Howardites volunteered to serve their country. In an effort to support them, Howard president Mordecai Johnson and Dr. James Nabrit formed the Committee on Howard Men and Women in the War. This committee regularly corresponded with Howard students in the military. It also sent care packages of books to the students. In 1964, Dr. Nabrit donated a collection of letters between Howard faculty and staff with the alumni serving in the military to the Moorland Foundation. In total, 164 letters were collected from various academic units across the campus. The letters cover the period from 1941 to 1946, the beginning of U.S. involvement in the war until the waning months of the U.S. presence. The stories contained in the letters provide a personal look into the lives of these alumni while in the service.

The following letters provide a brief snapshot into the experience of Howardites in World War II.

Station Hospital
Cp. San Luis Obispo, Calif.

15 March 1945

Dear Mr. Nabrit,

Sorry I couldn't attend Charter Day Exercises.

I receive the Alumni Bulletin regularly and look forward eagerly to the news it brings. I have been in the Army 18 mos., and have come in contact with many former classmates and Howard students. It always brings pleasant memories, to mind, to meet and chat. Somehow it helps the day along and that means so much to those of us in the Armed Forces.

I am an Army Dietitian and at present am the only one on this Post. My work is very interesting.
Enclosed is a small contribution to the scholarship fund.

I hope our boys will be coming home soon. We, here, offer a prayer for the many who cannot come back.
Yours truly,

Elgeina Bell
2nd Lt. MD.D

Hq., 95th ENGR REGT
APO 350 c/o Postmaster
New York City, N.Y.
Aug 14, 1944
Somewhere in France

My Dear Mr. Nabrit,

Several months ago when I received your very informative letter on Howard's activities and other Howardites, I promised to write you a long letter because at that time I didn't have ample time, however, since that time I have been moving so very fast until I have scarcely had too much time for personal correspondence. As you will note since my last letter, I have been moved from England to France.

The moss covered chimneys and side walls of the Buildings left standing, a very definite indication that the buildings were quite old. Some I'm sure dating back to the 16th century. The thatched roofs that still remain, remind one of a garden; springing up from the top. As a result of the warm rays of the sun (sunny France), wheat and corn may be seen sprouting. Evil springs from the dark core of the world and brings with it life, and things without flesh and blood, things void and begin to stir. This period of liberation is liken unto that of the Renaissance Period to the French people. Streams of moving columns of peasants may be seen filing by. They are returning to the ruined cities in which they once lived, only to find nothing but a heap of ruin and an occasional chimney, and a few pieces of furniture only to be salvaged. The French have had so many such similar interruptions in their civilization as a result of war. I suppose even the very young children have grown weary.

After all most of the fighting today, to my mind, is being done with much courage and fortitude regardless of the capacity, whether on the front or on the docks. I say this because not too many of us are represented in actual combat groups comparatively speaking, from the representation of colored troops in this theater, they are performing their duties willingly and with much proficiency, not stopping to ask what we are fighting for; well wouldn't it be kind of hard to say what we are fighting for at any rate? In the last war perhaps various answers such as this would be applicable: the French were fighting to keep the Germans away from Paris; the English didn't want them near the Channel; the Russians were trying to drive them back into their own country. Perhaps each little spot in Europe is looked upon with greedy eyes with every neighboring country always ready to plunge into a war of aggression or for defense of some traditional holding. I sometimes wonder where does the culture lie, on this side of the ocean or at home? I only believe there are many more monuments and museums erected abroad! From all latest reports of the war today, all five fronts are progressing according to schedule and plan; armored spearheads and tank columns make advances in France; liberators make progress in the Pacific; the Russians throw in crack regiments on their front, allied forces in Asia make advances and in Italy, Florence reported to have been cleared by the polis (unofficial), and flank the Gothic line. I sincerely hope by the time you have received this letter the Allies will have reached Paris, the Russians in Berlin and this phase of the war ended.

After all it does take from eight to eleven days for mail to reach the United States. When this gigantic task is over and the free people can resume their normal way of life, I suppose it will be like PUTTING DOWN A HEAVY WEIGHT.

A few of former Howardites that I have by chance been able to contact are as follow: 1st Lt Benjamin C. Smith, T. Sgt. Joan C. Houseit, S/Sgt. John T. Riley and Private Thomas H. Chase. Our Chaplain at the present time is 1st Lt. Lewis A. McGee although not a former member of Howard. He is no doubt known around D.C. Prior to Chaplain McGee, Captain Edward G. Carroll, former staff member of Morgan College.

At this time I wish to extend my very best wishes to all, and I hope that this year will bring one of the largest classes to Howard ever in history. I have planned to return to Howard and resume my studies after the war is over. I beg to remain.

Very sincerely,

T/Sgt.   Frederic F. Clanagan

31st WAC Hospital Co.
England General Hosp.
Atlantic City, N.J.

Dear Sirs:

I am a graduate of Howard University in the year 1944, June. This year as in the years past I have enjoyed looking forward to attending the annual Lincoln-Howard Thanksgiving game, and would like to attend again this year. Would it be possible for you to send me as soon as possible information concerning the game—where it will be, when it will be, and the price of admission. Will it be possible to get student rate? My roommate and two other WACs wish to attend also.

Please send me this information.

Here in the WACs I am in training as a student dietician and expect to receive my commission as a dietician by April of 1946. It has been both interesting and profitable for me to belong to this organization, for I have gained a variety of experiences in the field of dietetics that could not have been afforded me as a civilian. Just as now, I am working under a dietician who spent thirty (36) months overseas in a hospital where clinical diet therapy cases were varied and many; and she gives me as problems (homework) many of the actual cases that she was confronted with overseas. Such as this will be very beneficial to me when I am out in the field and in a responsible position.

You will hear from again soon.

Sincerely yours,
Essie Marie Crowell

Company "A"
APO-92-c/o PM
N.Y.C., N.Y.
1 Dec. 44

Secretary
Howard Univ.
Washington, D.C.

Dear Sir;
I received my Howard Bulletin and was exceedingly glad to hear from the Old School. Sitting here on the Front lines in Italy it helped for a nite to vanquish all the cares and woes of a Company Commander and believe me they are many. Back in the days of my years on the Campus, never did I believe then that at some later date I would be worried about whether my men would get Trench foot or some other strange disease. Or whether or not men would get fed today or tomorrow or even where we mite be in the next 24 hours. But here we are, myself and my officers, Constantly thinking about these things. Well do I now appreciate the days I spent on the Campus and the days of minor worries of whether or not I would be in school when the "Grass grows Greener."

There with me are many Howard Men. I'll try to name a few and what they are doing. First of all there is Lt Alfred L. Savoy who commands one of the platoons in my company. He is doing a fine job and many of his men have been recommended for the Silver Star. Lt. Harry S. Davis who is executive officer of Co. "B." same Regiment and same APO. Lt. George P. Thomas, 365 Inf. APO 92 c/o PM. N.YC., N.Y. He is Communication Officer. Lt. John Hunter, 365th Inf. Lt. Edgar McDonald, 365th Inf., Lt. Gordon, 371st Inf.; S/Sgt. Andrew J. Howard III, who is the Sergeant Major of the 1st Bn 371st Inf. and many others who I can't think of now. Those I have named are serving on the Front line with Infantry Units and they are certainly doing a fine job and should make those of Howard feel very proud of them. I am sure they would appreciate it if you could arrange it so that we could receive The School paper, "The Hilltop."

Give my regards to Deans Thurman and Hawkins and Mother Hopkins.

Edgar B. Felton,
Felton
c.o.
COA 371st Inf.
APO 92- c/o PM, N.Y.C, N.Y.

Co. 15 H.
Naval Training School (E.E. & R.M)
190 U. State St. Chicago Ill.
Jan 30, 1945

Dear Mr. Nabritt,

Last July, in Summer School, I thought I was on my way to a Bachelor's degree and then Med. School, however Uncle had other plans and I've been in the Navy since August. I was a student at Howard since the fall of 1942 and had really become attached to the place. Perhaps you remember me; I made a few excursions to your office while I was at Howard, generally as an Alpha representative trying to phenagle [sic] some compromise with the administration but at other times merely as a class representative seeking advice.

Since I've been in the Navy, my lot hasn't been too bad. I'm now in Radio Technician School stationed in Chicago. It's a ten month training course and very interesting. Only about eight Negroes have been admitted to this training and they're all still in training. It'll be Interesting to see what the Navy does with Colored radio technicians when they never had any before. This training program is very new itself. It didn't start until 1942. Previous to that, damaged radio or radar equipment was surveyed and repaired by civilians unless the repair was so minor that the radioman could fix it. Another former Howardite is here, Louis Giles. He graduated from Engineering School in '41 I believe. He has a brother Julian in Med. School.

The air of frivolity and lightheadedness that prevailed over Howard's campus is quite different from the attitude of the men here. By necessity every man is a student, and liberty on Wednesday nights and weekends is greatly appreciated. I wish I had taken my work a little more seriously while I was in school, but I suppose all the fellows in the service say the same thing. You'll realize that they meant it when this is over and they come back. If you see Dean West mention me to him and I hope the end of this war will result in an America with something of the liberalism that is Howard.

Sincerely,
Lester E. Florant '46

4 May 45

Dear Miss Henry,

I received the books last week. I and the rest of the boys are truly grateful for what you and Mrs. Dudley are doing to boost our morale and to keep us abreast of current events. Please excuse this late reply to the receipt of the books. I myself hate excuses, but at the time the books arrived, my outfit was constantly moving because we had the Germans retreating rapidly. We have caused all of the German Armies in Italy to surrender, not because of the lack of food, ammunitions or men, rather because we out fought them. When the Germans surrendered, it resembled a Roman holiday. They had plenty of horses, covered wagons, bicycles and all kinds of cars, including the American Fords and Army Jeeps. Now that we have finished here we are waiting for a new assignment—guard duty here in Italy, return to America, or go to the So. Pacific. We all hope it is not the latter. So, with good luck, we may see the next "White Christmas" in the U.S.A.

Perhaps we can repay you and Mrs. Dudley in the future.

yours,
Thaddeus H. Dobbs

April 15th 1943

Somewhere in the British Isles
American Red Cross for the Armed Forces

And now a word from me to you.... This article explains the procedures for the Red Cross Clubs in the British Isles. Our club is not listed but it operates on the same principles as the ones described in the article. It is named The American Red Cross Duchess Street Service Club. It accommodates 95 men for lodging. It is very cozy and comfortable—a real home-like atmosphere, open fires and attractive furnishings. There are nine American Red Cross persons and 35 British personnel, secretaries, cooks, maids, porters, receptionists etc. who are responsible for the operations, also a British person as manager. The club is usually filled to capacity. The Red Cross is very generous with funds for the comfort of American soldiers.

Signed; Geneva J. Holmes

Capt. Walton C. Jackson
0-15, 378, 2012, OM co T (a)
APO – 321, c/o PM., San Fran, Cal
2 May 1944

APPENDIX A

The Secretary
Howard University
Washington, D.C.

My Dear Mr. Nabrit,

The delightful newsletter dated 1 April 1944 from your office was a most unsuspected surprise and a great joy to me. Please be assured that such splendid efforts on your part are indeed a great inspiration to us Howardites who have been scattered to the four corners of the earth in a search for life and liberty and happiness.

That the President and the university community would excel in holding up its end of the war effort has never been doubted by all Howardites where-ever they may be. Also it is most encouraging to know that the student body, although its numbers are greatly depleted of matured male persons, is, never-the-less, progressing in a manner typical of Howard University students through out all the past years. The scholarship effort for needy students is highly commendable we who are oversees have run the gauntlet of travels in strong winds, war dangers, to searing demands of extreme climate and the stresses and strains of all the common emotions. But the hope that it all will lead to a hobbies life in a fairies land (turn to S.W.P.A.) is a constant inspiration.

Furloughs and paydays are the immediate highlights of the soldier's daily life. Take it from one who knows, a fifteen day furlough in Brisbane, Sidney, or Melbourne embraces all the exotic adventures and experiences and excitement that may come only with the heterogeneous masses of the large far eastern cities. The ingenious methods used by the soldier to dispose of or increase this [illegible] are sources of never ending encouragement. In truth "Aunt [illegible] Children" are miraculously successful in a game known as "galloping dominoes." Those who are well versed in its operation state that it is a very common diversion of ancient vintage.

Our out to this theatre our voyage upon the calm deep blue Pacific presented many opportunities to observe a multitude of strange awe inspiring examples of marine life. (Even though the sea menace cause constant fear among us all). The lofty mountains that we have seen are so tall that while the sun shines on the peaks rain clouds and rain are observed far below. Meanwhile we from afar in a pleasant many shot look on in wonder.

The dense storming jungle is an eternal mystery. Myriads of flying and creeping and crawling and biting and stinging things turn man's life into a tortuous passage. On the other hand the exaggerated tales of giant snakes and weird animals may be greatly discounted.

Mosquitoes!! Mosquitoes!! Oh these mosquitoes!! Following is a happening that has been authenticated by not a few GI's vig:

"There is a certain large species of mosquitoes about the size of humming birds commonly seen in New Guinea. One night a tribe of them fell upon a lonely unsuspecting G.I. in his tent, [illegible] him down and were tearing him apart bit by bit. There being so many of the flying tribe, a large number were unable to get their share of its booty. Therefore one ingenious fellow cried "hey fellows let's take this guy outside where all of us can get to him at the same time. But a few of the older heads angrily growled back, what and let those big mosquitoes outside, take him away!!"

Personal relationships between the Aussies, the damn Yankees (as we are called) and the natives are very cordial. The hospitality of the Aussies in the forward area and on the mainland is unlimited and sincere. As for the natives who are very intelligent and quick to learn, they have accepted the war and carry on in the most matter of the fact manner.

Every soldier is constantly alert to the many dangers. Woe be unto a man who is caught off his guard at any time. A soldiers operating procedure is that every man will have perfected at least six good ways offsetting getting to and into a foxhole. Only the true in heart can carry on while the weak soon fall by the wayside.

Yes, war is hell, but life is good. The lofty mountains, the boundless wastes, the cloudless skies, and the good earth. Are ever reminders of the minutia that is man. But as long as we have a mind, a body, a soul, a heart, and a spirit no obstacle is to hard to overcome.

Pursuant to the request in your letter, am enclosing a photo of me taken just after my promotion from 1ˢᵗ lieutenant to Captain. The picture was taken in a clearing located in an almost impassable jungle.

I close with sincere wishes for your food health and continued success.

Yours truly,
Walton C. Jackson
0-7575378
Captain QMC

A P 0 #93 Care Postmaster
San Francisco, California
23 April 1944

Dear Dr. Nabritt [sic]*:*

Your letter reached me today in a lonely South Pacific island. I read it by an eerie light that entered my bomb-proof shelter. And outside, where rain has fallen all day, I can hear the periodic accent of artillery fire.

I was particularly proud of the fact that the interesting letter I received was the suggestion of my friend and classmate, Otto McClarrin. Therefore, I am waiting no time in answering it.

The second paragraph of your letter was very suggestive. When you say, "...Close your eyes and return with us for a visit to old Howard...." you ask for something I do quite often. From this, spot 10,000 miles from home (and a mile from the Japs) nostalgia possesses me and I can see clearly the Long Walk leading to Clark Hall's east entrance. One of the vivid memories I shall always keep with me is the one of Howard's Campus in springtime. In fact, without seeming unappreciative, let me tell you that your letter served to remind me how pitifully futile is life in our time.

Here on this island I see natives who heretofore have been the subject of sociological studies. They live in abject poverty. But they live in peace. Around them some of the finest specimen of civilized human beings are dying and rotting away. Not far from where I am writing mortal combat is taking place between men of my unit and the Japanese. That combat is characterized by a brutal savagery unsurpassed even in the heyday of cannabalism [sic].

But let me assure you that even war has its compensations. To me, one of these is the unique experience of working in areas where hitherto men have by-passed as inaccessible. The plant life is extremely interesting. The insects and reptiles here could be the subject of a lifetime of study.

For instance, the spot where we now make our camp on this island has never been inhabited before its occupation by the army. Its selection speaks well for our army intelligence. It was once virgin jungle. Now there run through it several network of roads.

In my own outfit there are many Howardites and Washingtonians. 1st Lt. Wilbur Goodwin, Howard '36 is with our Anti-Tank Company. 1st Lt. Conway B. Jones of Washington is in command of a rifle company. Incidentally, Jones was recommended for the Combat Infantryman Badge for a little work he did on a Jap. It seems that this Tojo-man saw Jones and his 1st Sgt. He took several shots at Jones. He missed. Jones sided behind a tree and asked one of his men to hand him an MI rifle: the Garand to you. With one shot at 400 yds he transformed this live sniper into a good dead Jap. This experience, and many others has shown us that a Japanese soldier is a poor shot. He is at his worse when he has to fire from long distances. He is only dangerous when he can ambush or otherwise bewilder green troops.

We have with us also Lt. Lemuel Penn, Howard '34 who is with a Heavy Weapons Company. 1st Lt. Oswald Monroe, Howard is with another regiment occupying an island nearby. So is 1st Lt. Chappell C. Cochrane, Howard B. S. and A. M. (Chemistry) and 1st Lt. Tim Irving, Howard, '34.

More Howardites here are: 1st Lt. Eric Edwards (recently promoted to 1st). 1st Lt. Wendell McConnell, Howard A.B. and LL.B. McConnell is Battalion S-2 (intelligence) for one of our battalions. He was the first Negro officer to go on patrol activities against the Japs here. Everyone speaks highly of his work. I have no doubt that along with Jones he ranks as among the best line officers in the division.

My own work is in supply. I like this phase of military duty; but so far I have not been given any definite assignment. This brings me to the distasteful aspect of my military career. I am sure you are quite familiar with the complaints of colored officers.

Recently I read Agnes Meyer's article in the Washington Post. *She certainly covered the ground well. She is right when she says that the treatment of colored soldiers has shaken his faith in the validity of their military service. I confess that I am one of those who by now has not only reached that attitude; but I am also doubting the future of the Negro in America. My experiences in the army have not been pleasant. In my capacity as an officer with colored troops I have had the opportunity to see the ultimate results of denial of basic rights to Negroes.*

A Negro who is denied the right to a decent education and who is frustrated in the development of his character and personality by discrimination becomes at maturity a dangerous blend of civilized and atavistic tendencies. Many of them are susceptible to moods of depression. And the requirements of army life in preparation for combat produce adverse psychological adjustment. Only today I spent a large part of the day discussing the matter with a hospital psychiatrist.

To some extent—and with important reservations—I am incline to agree with the statement made recently by Secretary of War Stimson: his letter to Mr. Fish of New York. The question I ask is: What is the cause of the Negro's failure to grasp technological requirements of modern combat? Certainly no well-informed person will say that the Negro does not possess the mental capacity. Evidence to the contrary is overwhelming. My own conclusion is that the American Negro is a product of the immorality of the Americans by legislation and social custom denied him his basic rights. As a result, the Negro soldier lacks an indispensable element required in combat: inspiration. I was just wondering how can any person familiar with Georgia, Mississippi, or Texas expect a colored soldier from any of those states to feel inspired to fight for the democracy he has known there? Well...

I want to thank you for the copy of your letter, Dr. Nabritt [sic]. Will you please forward my address to Otto. I can't understand what he did to deserve an army sentence in Mississippi? Tell him he deserves foreign duty pay for that tour.

Censorship regulation prohibit my telling you where I am now stationed. I can tell you where I've been. I arrived here from Guadalcanal nearly a month ago. I like it much better here. However, I do hope that our stay here will be short.

Please remember me to my friends at Howard: Dean West, Dean Elliott, the Library Staff, Dean Hawkins, and others who might ask about me. And above all, let me have another letter from you.
Sincerely,
George N. Leighton

Appendix A

"Somewhere in the Moluccas"
20 June 1945

Mr. James M. Nabritt
Howard University
Washington, D.C.

Dear Mr. Nabritt:
It is only proper that the many students of Howard University report to you their experiences in this war. Right now we are in a stage of this important event when it should be well to summarize what we have seen and heard. I feel that a man in your position would be able to put together the varied experiences of Negroes who have served in the armed forces throughout the world.

More than a year has past since I first wrote to you from Bougainville in the British Solomons. During this time I have had the good fortune of visiting many of our bases in this area. From these outposts have gone the troops and the supplies that have made certain the eventual victory over the Japanese. In the midst of all this activity has been numerous Negro troops performing-work in a manner that would make any group proud.

I have seen Negro engineers building roads over which important supplies have gone from depot to ships. I have seen Negro quartermaster battalions organize and operate depots that supplied frontline troop in contact with the enemy thousands of miles away. I have seen ordnance companies composed of colored troops handling vital ammunition supply. Then, I have seen Negro combat troops doing their share.

But if the truth be told in its proper light, the Negro's contribution to the winning of the war is in the field of service and supplies. That contribution will never be properly evaluated. As I see it, there are two reasons. One is that those who have the facts do not consider it important enough to warrant separate study. The second reason is that Negro writers who have the interest, and who do think it is important to appraise the Negroes contribution to the war, do not have the intelligence to sift the important facts from the trivial.

This last reason would to a great extent explain the recent discussions in the American press—Negro and White—concerning the success of Negro combat troops. On the part of the Negro press there is a morbid emphasis being put on the exploits of combat troops. This is an unfair attitude toward the many colored soldiers who through no fault, of theirs are now serving with the ASF. On the part of the White press there is a policy to ignore the contribution the Negro is making. Lately, however, there seems to appear more articles on Negro troops. Most of these are sanely and carefully written. Yet there is much that could be done if more intelligent Negroes would take a hand in this problem.

I can tell you that here among our troops the average colored soldier is becoming more and more disgusted with the pitifully asinine reports that are printed each week in the Afro-American, Pittsburgh Courier, *and* Chicago Defender. *Not only are those articles inaccurate. They go so far as to print blatant falsehoods that make the colored troops the laughing stock of the white soldiers who know the true facts. A recent case in point is the June 9 issue of the* Pittsburgh Courier *that describes the action of a detachment from my regiment. It was written by Billy Rowe, the ex-gossip columnist turned war correspondent. That paper is now going the rounds among the white officers who are using it for the joke that it is. Even the former Howard student who commanded the troops in that routine movement was amused at the childish sensationalism used in reporting that event. Negro editors and writers don't seem to realize that actually they have fumbled a great opportunity. If you would now read the reports from Italy that appeared in the Negro press during the winter months of this year you would wonder why the War Department insisted on keeping the American 5th Army in that area when the 92nd Division was allegedly wiping out the Werhmacht. And if a review of the May–June 1944 issues of the* Afro *and the* Pittsburgh Courier *were made, it would appear ridiculous why the War Department kept other troops on Bougainville while we were there. According to those reports we were wiping out the Japs faster than they could be produced in incubators. All this nonsense when read by those who know the truth only reflect the lack of depth and maturity that characterizes the Negroes who today are sitting in the editors' chairs of the Negro Press. The net result is that the returning veteran will have less faith in what appears in Negro papers than heretofore. It is unfortunate but true.*

Quite often I like to think that someday we will dedicate a student Union Hall at Howard University in memory of the thousands of negro soldiers who gave their lives in this war. On its façade I would like to see a sculptured mural depicting the contribution they made toward victory. We should show in bold relief the Negro stevedore as I saw him in Finschafen with sweat on his face and his rifle nearby to right off the Japs. We should show the Negro engineer grading oil airfield runways while mounted beside him is his anti-aircraft gun with he used to shoot down Japanese Zeros. And we should put there adequate tribute to the thousands of Negro quartermasters and port battalion men who pushed forward the supplies that have gone toward winning the war. Then, in proper emphasis, we should show the Negro Infantryman and Air Corp personnel who have done their share.

I shall be waiting again for more of your interesting Howard letters.

Sincerely,
George N. Leighton
Capt., 25th Infantry

HQ. Det. 1390th Service Unit
(Special Training Unit)
Holabird Signal Depo
Baltimore, Maryland
15 December 1943

Dear President Johnson:

This cold night finds me alone in the Day Room for the 1390th S.U. That is surprising. The place is usually bustling with life, and I prefer noise in the neighborhood for letter writing. It gives me a sense of being in the center of the intensity of things—a sense that all good letter possess.

With a makeshift of a magic carpet, I'll take you over some of the main ground I've covered since I left the University. I was transported to Camp Lee (near Petersburg), Va. in a bus. The bus was easy-riding, and the trip was quiet. Only one thing worried me: the expressions on the faces of the men, as I watched them with side glances, full stares, and querying looks in the mirror, were deeply puzzling. I could have understood anger or loneliness or simple despair. But most of these men showed hollowness— absolute hollowness, as though they were the secret panels in a thick wall. I reasoned: "It's because they do not like to leave the people they have just so tearfully told goodbye." Or, "because they are Negroes and are wondering if this is in any sense their war." Or: "most of them really deep down realize the great futility of killing before one does what must be done with one's world." But there was more to their hollowness than that. These men had the hollowness of wondering if anyone really cared for their personal, particular discomfiture and sacrifice. They were each a nation going to war. They would not have gone by themselves, and they could not feel that the gigantic forces that set them as individuals in motion had any cause for whirling at that time.

In Camp Lee, I was the commonest of common soldiers. I did grounds police, kitchen police, fire guard, "the works." I "fell out "in front of the Company Orderly room on the double. I learned the true meaning of the adage: "It never rains (snows, develops high winds, etc. etc.) in the Army; It only rains on the Army." Though I didn't smoke I had to pick up other people's cigarette butts and match stems. I learned the meaning of community by helping to pay for the mistakes or arrogance of people in my unit when only one or two of 200 men were at fault.

It all reminded me of the opening of Walt Whitman's <u>Drum Taps</u>. Bad as war was to him (a Quaker by ancestry), he could see that it taught men comradeship and devotion for common causes more dramatically than anything previously used. It made men see each other's faults. It made men rise and fall together. It concentrated their personal strength to a community purpose.

If only someone could devise a highly dramatic peacetime enterprise to do those things as well—
I took the Army Tests and did fairly well. I was classified as a Teacher and sent here to help prepare illiterate and semi-literate men for Army Service. As I work, the main thing I think of is that thousands of men here will not be in the absolute dark any more—ever. I close my eyes to the fact that success here means more cannon fodder sooner.

The steps in the system here are about as follows:

1. Receive the men from the Induction Reception Center.

2. Test them to find if any are 4th grade caliber in reading or writing; if any, order them sent immediately out for training.

3. Send the others to whatever level the multiple test scores show them fit for.

4. Follow them as they go from level to level; if they fail once, examine their backgrounds carefully and make recommendations; if twice, call them in for highly personal, thorough, systematic individual examinations.

5. Recommend for discharge from the Army all hopeless cases.

6. Keep close records on everything.

Although I came here to teach, my first stop was in the office of the Personnel Consultant (who is in charge of the system described), and there I have remained. I have done (at least once) everything the variegated job calls for. I am now the chief record-keeper and statistician, but at times— tomorrow for example—I devote myself mainly to giving the Individual Examinations. I work hard, but about half as hard as I did "on the Hilltop high."

And I am worried about those kids, Mr. President. From what I hear, they aren't getting nearly enough attention. I wish it were possible for me to do this job and one there, too. I'm trying to keep in touch with key students, but I'm not happy about their opportunities.

I can't tell you everything in one letter, and so this rush of words must stop. Oh yes, will you please see if there's any way for you to arrange for me to get my check for Remedial English I did in A.S.T.P. last summer. I hadn't expected it before now, but I was counting on it for Christmas. It seems to have struck a severe snag. And that's bad news, considering that the Army's taking out for two months' dependency allowance and three months insurance has caused me to be "redlined" (get no pay) so far.

Please accept from me to you and Mrs. Johnson my heartiest Christmas wishes. I hope to see you early next year at the latest.

I'm not alone anymore!!

Prvt. John Lovell, Jr.

❧———❧

24 April 44

Dear Mr. Nabrit,

Hell no I didn't receive the January Bulletin—nor the one before that, nor the other dozen or so before that. I've known Otto for eight years now. It's the first idea he's had worth its weight on paper. It's a good one.

You suggested that I close my eyes and return with you for a visit to old Howard. Of course I couldn't figure how I could close my eyes and read the letter too but by cheating a little with a wink here and a squint there. It was just about like walking the campus again.

I have always contended that Howard is somewhat unique among universities in the way it refuses to let you forget it despite time and space. Whenever I want to inject myself with a good dose of nostalgia I follow your prescription to the letter—close my eyes and return—not home nor to church nor to "U" Street—but to Howard. I can really make myself miserable.

Seems to me as though I have sent a dollar or so to the University for the Scholarship Fund. That was well over a year ago now. I hadn't forgotten the university but the fund was certainly lost to me. An occasional bulletin would remedy that. The last one I saw was on the Louisiana November (last spring) in the hands of a man who did very, very, little reading or writing. He asked me to read parts of it for him. I founds a picture of myself in it. Must have been pretty old.

I observe that the university is struggling through an extremely crucial period in its history. Women running a student council and the Hilltop!! I wouldn't be surprised that they are presiding over the classes too. Next thing you know they'll be flying airplanes, voting, and drilling with the A.S.T.P. Good luck to them. I'm sure they're doing the good job—(considering their innate handicaps)

I hope to be in D.C. at the end of next month. I'll drop in on you. Meantime, I'll appreciate the Bulletin's you've been hoarding up there.

Yours,
[Wendell] *Lucas*

25 October 44

Dear "Prof"

Just In case your news bulletin would be interested your truly finds himself way down South in New Orleans. How successful class 31 will be in making an officer and a gentleman out of me remains to be seen—come December 20th. If you have an extra copy of the latest Bulletin I'd like to have one so as to catch up on the other Howardites in the Service.

Facts you probably know: Randolph "Brick" Bailey was promoted from Cp2 to WO (2G) in SW Pacific with 93rd Div. JAC HQ....Capt.

Cleve Jackson relates from his outpost in Pacific that he'd rather be in the infantry; at least they have more than a prayer for protection. Lt. Courtland C. Bivens (St. Louis) hasn't written for a month which may indicate that he has finally reached Paris and is either busy or having his afternoon tea on the sidewalks.

So far my treatment in OCS has been superb. There is not one iota of detectable discrimination. The officers go out of their way to make it plain to all cooperation is a by-word in the Transportation Corps. Colonel Ackerman would not hesitate to wash a man out who openly spoke the word "nigger."

From what I've learned about Transportation in general there are some unexplored angles so far as the solution of some of your common carrier problems are concerned. Maybe I'll be back on the campus and we can get together for a discussion.

Give my regards to all who may inquire.

Sincerely Yours

Lundy

March 11, 1945
Somewhere in N. Burma
Capt. G.E. Marshall
335 Station Hospital
APO #689 c/o Pm
New York, NY

Mr. James M. Nabrit, Jr

While visiting one of my fellow officers here at our hospital, I spied a Howard Univ. Bulletin for July 1944 and my interest was immediately aroused. Taking time out, called "gold bricking" in the army, I sat and read and dreamed of my wonderful days at H.U., now but a memory. My wife, the former Alberta Ann Gibson, also a Howardite is living with her parents in Chicago. Brother, Dr. Caesar L. Marshall has obtained additional time from the army to take a surgical residency at St. Mary's Infirmary in St. Louis.

My younger sister Miss Hope Marshall hopes to enter Freedmen's Nursing School in the near future, while sister Katherine Ann Marshall a graduate of the 1937 Dental Hygiene course is married to Cpt. Paul Brown, AA 4 now in Italy.

Once I was commissioned, things really began to happen. After finishing Carlisle Medical Field Service School, I proceeded to H. Huachuca and remained in the M.D R.P. Sta. Hosp. one of the all Negro units of this sort in the Army, I was forthcoming and lo and behold they were packed ready to ship out. So there I was, no time for a furlough or anything on my way. Our officer personnel, which included Howardites H. Clarence Hinton, M.C., Lt. Marvin Fisk, M.C., Capt. Henry Washington, M.C., and Army C.O. Major Wilber Strickland, M.C. flew overseas from La Guardia Field New York, early in August. Our first stop was in Newfoundland and from there to the neutral Azores Islands owned by Portugal. A most paradoxical situation existed there—an allied and a German airfield sat side by side with only a small rise and a distance of about one mile between them. Some of the men there said that they spied on one another but that was all.

The next hop took us over water for ten straight hours and placed us in Casablanca, N. Africa. Sorry to say the Humphrey Bogart film flattered this place it is truly filthy and teeming with all manner of human debris. I was glad when we left for Cairo, Egypt two days later. This is a most modern and beautiful city very clean and pleasant. While there we visited the Sphinx and Pyramids it was a wonderful experience and I was thrilled. After spending three delightful days in Egypt we were off again, eight hours brought us to Tripoli, hot dusty desert land still bearing the mark of Rommel's hasty retreat. The hanger resembled a sieve it was so full of holes and wrecked tanks, trucks and armor of all sorts was in evidence. We found out that our next stop would be Karachi, India and we weren't disappointed. This local has the best climate in all of India. Refreshing trade winds, cool the days and at night, one is quite comfortable under a blanket. Five delightful days were spent there with a Negro ordinance outfit which had been overseas thirty two months. Their morale was wonderful and they were happy and proud to see some Negro officers. It seems that the white G.I's in competing for local female talent, had told the girls that the colonel lads had tails, were rapist and coalies in the states and that there were no negro officers in the U.S. Army. I understand they had quite a row after we left.

This was too good to last and we were on our way again. Assam, India being our destination which is two thousand miles across India. The most beautiful and spectacular sight of the whole trip came at 2 am one morning when we flew over the Taj Mahal and viewed it by moonlight with the entire tiresome trip. Once is Assam we convoyed up the Lelo Road built almost entirely by negro engineer and driving by Negro Q.M.C. drivers (90%) to our present site in N. Burma.

I believe I'm right in saying I'm the first A.S.T. officer to come overseas (Aug 24th) and the first in my class to make captain (Feb. 18th) If I'm wrong please inform me. I forgot to tell you Lt. Andre Tweed is also with this outfit. Thanks a lot for listening to my rambling. I wrote to my Dean but he hasn't seen fit to answer. I hope I can hear from someone back at my alma mater.

Yours Truly,
Capt. George A. Marshall, Q.C.

James M. Nabrit, Jr
Office of the Secretary
36020277
Howard University

Pvt. John H. Marshall
HQ. Btry 999 M.F.A.
Washington, D.C.
A.P.O. 403 70 Pm NYC

May 1, 1945

Dear Howardite: Please accept my thanks for the most interesting letter sent to alumni everywhere. This battalion debarked upon Utah Beach, France complete equipment and personnel, the battalion started to move with the third U.S. Army in hot pursuit of the fleeing German force and [illegible] days marched more than 180 miles in [the] face of armed resistance, occupying thirteen positions. From the position at Arracourt and at Mantes, Messi Court, occupied on the infantry outpost line, over 10 tons of ammunition were exploded in helping the 79th Division established a bridge lead over the Seine River. This action sealed off the last escape route for Seventh German Army, which had been evicted by the swift advance of the Americans. During this time every night, the Seine was lighted by the heaviest concentration of artillery ever assembled.

After this offensive, positions were occupied near Chambley and Gorze. Before reaching these positions the battalion passed through Verdun, battle site of World War I. From there positons, which were beyond a doubt the hottest for our ground offense and wire crews, fire was placed on forts surrounding Metz. The battalion then moved south, supporting the 79th Division and the Red French River. Ending a period of general support near Lureville, the battalion again joined in the pursuit and destruction of routed German forces culminating in the capture of the important city Sarrebourg and after crossing the Vosges Mountains, took Savene and finally the Rhine City of Strasbourg. In one of these positions, Baker Battery was the most forward and [illegible] trained artillery of the Allied Armies on the western front. Near Bitale, one platoon of Baker moved forward on short notice and aided materially in the neutralization of Pt. Simserhof, an important point in the maginot line. Nearby twenty-five hundred rounds were expended in one of the most daring and spectacular advances made by the allies.

Next came the battle of the Colmar pocket, were by aggressive American and French forces. Since that time the battalion has crossed the Rhine River twice.

24th Inf. Med. Det.
APO 93 c/o P.M.
San Francisco, Calif.
May 29, 1944

Office of the Secretary
Howard University
Washington, D.C.

My Dear Sir:

The letter accompanying your questionnaire was a sources of great pleasure to those of us from Howard who are serving here. We sat around in our dug outs and for a brief time were able to forget the strain and unpleasantness of the job we are doing here. You may be assured that such a letter is very welcome here.

There are quite a few alumni of Howard serving over here in the South Pacific. All are doing fine job upholding the traditions and reflecting the training we received there, despite extremely unpleasant conditions.

Besides the usual factors that place great strain on men at the front during war, the colored officers here have a very bitter and insidious presences put on them by prejudice and discrimination…because of a lack of rank, they are powerless to improve the condition to any extent. As a [illegible] they get an express of dangerous assignments and missions and of course receive no promotions above 1ˢᵗ Lieut. In the line regardless of merit.

In spite of these serious handicaps, they are doing a job that their race and their school can justly be proud of.

I along with Capts. D.P. Gibson, Claude D. Walker and George J. Thomas send fond regards and best wishes for continued service and prosperity of Howard U.

Sincerely Yours,
Robert W. McDaniel
Capt. M.C.

Station Hospital
C.R.W. Camp
Florence, Ariz.

12 May 1945

My Dear Mr. Nabrit:

For some time now I have wanted to send you a note thank you and all those who are responsible for sending the "University Bulletin" to me and many other Howardites.

No, you will never know how much it does for the morale of the men and women in the services when we get the news about so many who we know so well.

When I received the last bulletin I read it through before stopping. I learned that whereabouts of so many who I had been wondering about. Then, I passed it on to the bulletin board.

I have been in Arizona three years now and I seem to be stuck here. But for more than two years we had the 92nd, 93rd, 372nd and other outfits who have gone on to do a great job over there.

Now as a result of their efforts we are serving two German Prisoners of war and it has been a great experience.

I am learning German now, sorry I did not take it as the University.

I think you know the rest up here. The female officers are the only Negroes around here. We have no contact with Negroes at all. Be we are doing well. We have no trouble, there is no discrimination on the post, it's not allowed. Our patients are white G.I.s and P.W.'s all male officers are white. We receive the respect that is due us from all personnel.

We regret very much that the discrimination in the town around here is awful. We pray that soon we can walk into any restaurant, or soda fountain and be served food and drink. And to think any of these P.W.s can go any place and be served. On this part they get the best of everything.

You must be getting ready for commencement now. I wish that I could be there. The picture of the chapel on the cover of the last bulletin is most beautiful.

Thanks again for remembering us and keeping the good work on the home front.

Respectfully,
Lt. Lucia A. Pley, A.N.C

Sunday 9:30 PM

Mr. Nabrit:

Here's the material that you asked for—hope you can use some of it.... Please excuse the paper & whatever else is not correct....I'll leave it to you to "fix up."
And oblige,
Anastasia E. Scott

Miss Anastasia E. Scott, daughter of Rev. & Mrs. T. Leslie Scott of Roanoke, Va. Who has recently returned from England has been engaged in Military Welfare activities the American Red Cross, for the past two years.... [S]ome of the cities where she was stationed and which she had the privilege of visiting were London, Liverpool, Bristol, Salisbury, Leicester, Cheltenham, Torquay, Oxford, Stratford-on Avon & Cardiff.
It was in Liverpool that Miss S. had her first intensive experience with British Colored People. She found these people strikingly different from American Negroes—due largely to the difference in environment that the two peoples have been exposed to. However these people were found to be very charming and more than eager to follow the pattern of their American Sisters in the matters of manners, appearance and behavior. Many of these

girls proved to be delightful and satisfactory hostesses in the American Red Cross Clubs that were located in the areas where the British Colored population is concentrated.

Cardiff, South Whales has the largest colored population in Great Britain. This city is a veritable melting pot of various nationalities. For this reason it is an unrivaled locality for a sincere student of Sociology in addition to being an un-paralleled field for well trained & eager Social Workers to practice their profession. Community Organization Group Work and Case Work could be done there with unlimited satisfactions.... [T]he most colored population of Cardiff is the result of seamen from all parts of the world mating with English Women. Here is found the offspring of W. Indian & W. African fathers and English Mothers. Another racial admixture is the "Maltese"—very dark people with straight black hair. These people have resulted from African-[illegible] combinations....There are many Arabs in Cardiff and very beautiful people they are, but so bound by their religious convictions that their problem of adjustment is greatly intensified. The sheik (pronounced Shake) holds forth in a very dignified house of worship better known as the "Mosque." Added to these people are the off-spring of Chinese-English & Greek-English unions.

Bristol was the source of great interest to Colored Americans for, years ago it was one of the chief slave auctioning marts of the world and one of the remaining vestiges of that cruel and sorrowful era is the now famous "Black Boy Hill."

Miss S. had the privilege & pleasure of meeting several English women engaged in Social Work. These women had not had the opportunity for formal training in S.S. but were intelligent in England. This project gave temporary shelter & aid to unmarried war-mothers. The remuneration for welfare work in England, falls, woefully behind that received in the U.S.A.

One is quite unable to fully appreciate the ideals of a democracy until one sees at first hand the undemocratic form of government....However no article about England should be completed without mention that the British people of all classes accepted. The colored American unreservedly accept what insidious propaganda had been spread previously to our appearance in a given town or area. And where our work necessitated our remaining in said areas for a sufficient length of time—this attitude of pre-judgement was to a large extent changed.

Those who have been fortunate enough to go abroad with the American Red Cross and have enriched by the contacts as well as by the heartaches consider it an invaluable continuation of their education and will be better able to serve their country and their race in the post-war world.

(Miss S. recd. Her Group Work & Social Work Training at George Williams College & Loyola University in Chicago, Ill. In private life she is the wife of Herbert L. Dudley, prominent Detroit Attorney & also a Howard Graduate.)

29ᵗʰ S.S. Co.
APO #93
Los Angeles 52, Cal.
23 September 43

Hello folks

How goes your half of the world? My half is o.k. I'm now stationed at the desert training center at Camp Clipper, California. It's quite warm here during the day—only about 130°. Here's a good example of this heat! One day my commanding officer bought a thermometer which registered the usual 120° about 3 o'clock in the afternoon. I went to check the temperature and found the thermometer broken. Temperatures here have been recorded as high as 157°. Early in the morning it is so cold that I shiver under two blankets.

I have escaped the heat twice by spending 2 weekends in Los Angeles—about 200 miles from camp. I was there this past weekend. I really had a wonderful time. Saturday nite I went out in Hollywood to a C.B.S. Broadcast featuring Ronald Coleman, Lena Horne, Bing Crosby, Bob Hope, Jascha Heifetz, Rise Stevens, Robert Benchley and many other of the Hollywood stars. I also went to the Hollywood Canteen where I was fed and autographed by many stars. I left the canteen and went to the Hollywood nite club and sat at the same table with Lena Horne, At 1:30 am I went to see "So Proudly We Hail"—a very good picture. Sunday I went horseback riding and down to see the pacific. Monday *morning I saw Gary Cooper and Ingrid Bergman in "For Whom the Bell Tolls." It was <u>super excellent</u>. It will not be released at popular places before 1945.*

Los Angeles is really o.k. for me and the soldiers really can enjoy themselves there very inexpensively and at the same duck all this dust and heat.

While I was stationed at Ft. Huachuca, I spent three week-ends in Mexico two in Nogales and one in Aqua Prieta. I saw two very exciting bull-fights and my Spanish really came in handy. Incidentally, I am now teaching Spanish to a few of the fellows of my company.

How goes everything at Howard U? I really miss the campus and all the activities. I understand that all the graduating seniors who were called into the service were given complimentary "Bisons." However, I did not receive one. Will one of you please see that I get one, even if I have to pay for it? Thanx a lot. I would also like to get the Howard Bulletins.

You know—the army is not nearly as bad as I had once pictured it, and I'm actually enjoying it. My work is very interesting and the experience has profited me greatly. Realizing that conflict is international, and that every individual on the home and fighting fronts must play his part. I am sure that the day of retribution is not too far off and all the united nations and perhaps the world will live in peace and tranquility and all men and nations shall better understand each other.

Please write me. You know mail means a lot to soldiers, so please let me answer the mail call.

With thoughts of Howard, I remain
Sincerely,
Rollin

2nd Bn Hq Co 370th Inf
APO 92 c/o Postmaster
New York, NY
May 9, 1945

Dear Dr. Nabrit,

Your recent Howard newsletter was received a short time ago. Allow me to express my deep appreciation for the consideration that you and your office have shown in keeping the Howard men and women informed about Howard and other Howardites. Your bulletins, too, have been received with great enthusiasm and read with interest. Although my affiliations listed with the University was as an AST Trainee, I can not help feel myself a member of the Howard family.

Since coming overseas, I have had the good fortune to meet and work with many Howard men. Ours have been most wholesome and for me most profitable associations. It is not without heart felt gratitude that we so often turn our thoughts to dear ole Howard.

Being a part of the 92nd Division and having fought against the stubborn Nazi enemy. I am more convinced now than ever that our tasks which await us at home are to be met with great courage. It is to great institutions like Howard that we are looking to for guidance and strength of purpose in order to make noble ideals living realities.

My experiences here in Italy have been many and varied. My observations of the brutal realities of war have been heart rending. We can but trust that those in whose hands our destiny lies will deliver us to better days. Thank you again for making life in combat more bearable.

Sincerely,
Jerry

CONSTITUTION OF THE PROMETHEANS

(Let it be known that this constitution is temporary in nature and is to continue in force only until such time as a sufficient number of the members can assemble to adopt a more comprehensive document)

ARTICLE I. TITLE AND TYPE OF ORGANIZATION:

Organized under the title of THE PROMETHEANS, this title being derived from the Greek God Prometheus, who represented light and power, it is our intention to act as a guiding light and guiding power for the men in the AST at Howard University. The Prometheans is to function as a non-profit organization.

ARTICLE II. MEMBERSHIP:

Section 1. Eligibility to become a charter member of THE PROMETHEANS is, at present, restricted to any person who had attended an Engr. term or part of term as a member of the 2515th S.U. A.S.T.P. as of March 8, 1944.

Section 2. Honorary memberships will be issued to any person receiving two-thirds majority vote of all members of the organization.

ARTICLE III. ORGANIZATION SET-UP:

Section 1. Due to the location of the various members of the organization, it has become necessary to devise an extraordinary organizational set-up.

Section 2. The organizational officers shall consist of a Chairman, and a Sergeant-at-Arms.

Section 3. The organization is divided into a number of major units, regimental groups, which are presided over by two co-chairmen who are aided by a corresponding secretary.

Section 4. Each major unit is further subdivided into a number of minor units—battalion groups—which are presided over by two co-chairmen, who are assisted by a corresponding secretary.

Section 5. Each unit shall have an additional secretary who will take notes of the business of his unit.

Section 6. Each unit shall have a Sergeant-at-Arms who will preserve order under the direction of the presiding officer.

Section 7. The presiding officers shall preside at all meetings and shall enforce the constitution and by-laws.

Section 8. It shall be the duty of the secretary to preside over any meeting in the absence of the presiding officers.

Section 9. The unit corresponding secretary will act in the capacity of unit reporter.

Section 10. Until such time as the organization can come together as a body, the organization will be directed by an Organizational Coordinator. This position is now being held by an honorary member, Dr. MERZE TATE.

ARTICLE IV. MEETINGS:

Meetings will be held at such time as the unit officers deem it necessary and possible to call them.

ARTICLE V. QUORUM:

One-third of the members of a unit shall constitute a quorum for the transaction of business.

ARTICLE VI. AMENDMENTS:

This constitution may be amended by an announcement of the proposed amendment and a two-thirds vote of all the members of the organization; the vote being taken at least a month after the announcement of the proposed amendment:

BY-LAW

Section 1. By a two-thirds vote at any regular meeting the next regular meeting may be cancelled.

Section 2. The following shall be the order of business which shall be subject to change at any meeting by a two-thirds vote.

a. Call to order and roll call.

b. Reading, correction, and adoption of minutes of the previous meeting.

c. Unfinished business.

d. Reports of committees.

e. New business.

f. Collection of dues.

g. Adjournment

Section 3.

All payments shall be sent in the form of a money order or cashier's check to:

The Prometheans

c/o Dr. MERZE TATE

Howard University

Washington, D. C.

c. Authority has been vested in Dr. Merze Tate to control and supervise all business transactions, if approved by the Honorary advisory Board.

Section 4. Any measure which requires the vote of a proportion of the members of the organization may be acted upon by absentee ballot, provided that every member is furnished a ballot.

Section 5. The rules contained in Robert's RULES OF ORDER shall govern the organization in all cases to which they are applicable, and in which they are not inconsistent with the constitution and by-laws of the organization.

Section 6. These by-laws may be amended by at least a week's previous announcement of the proposed amendment and by a two-thirds vote of the members of the organization.

Section 7. Tenure of office will terminate at the time officers are elected under a permanent constitution.

NOTE:

This constitution was drawn up by Pfc Thaddaeus H. Hobbs, Pfc Rupert Hoover, and Pfc Otis F. Hicks, all of the 1st Battalion, 371st Infantry.

ANNEX

Whenever a majority of 60 of the members of the Prometheans vote to discontinue the offices of Organizational Coordinator and Comptrollers of Funds, the incumbents of these offices will immediately turn over to the Executive Council the funds that have accrued to the credit of the Prometheans. Thereupon the Comptrollers of Funds will cease to have any official connection with and legal and financial responsibility to the Prometheans.

Until such time as states above, no funds, except those necessary for operating expenses of the organization, shall be withdrawn from the treasury.

POEMS

To the Unknown Soldier
By Lorenzo J. Greene, Howard Class of 1924
November 1921

What means this sad yet gorgeous sight?
What means these flowers so rare?
Is all this splendor, all this pomp,
For one dead soldier there?

Who is this warrior bold deceased
What glory does he claim?
What honor to his country brought
That merits him this fame?

What valiant deed did he perform
On Flanders' reeking strand?
Was he like mighty Ajax, chief
Of some heroic band?

Did he into the battle's din
Rush in midst shot and shell
And stay until he lifeless sank
Amid that raging Hell?

What matter what of honor, fame,
He had his country brought?
What matter whether in the strife
Great deed of arms he wrought?

Think not of glory—but a breath!
But think of what he gave:
Ambition, loved ones, even life,
His native land to save.

In him a grateful nation shrines
Her nameless heroes lost:
Reveres her sons who with their life
Paid war's supremest cost.

This tribute breathes a nation's prayer,
That war fore'er may cease:
The o'er this bleeding earth may dawn
A day of lasting peace

—Reprinted from the *Howard University Record*, March 1924

On the Death of a Friend
By Florence A. Whitehead (sister of a Promethean)

When death came to our dear friend
On whom all nations could depend,
Shocked and grieved, we shed tears
To be remember through the years.

He gave his life to win the peace
Forgetting God on him had lease
His friendship and kindness were shared by all,
The Great, the meek on him could call.

One of our few leaders born
Who made it a practice not to scorn,
The Weak, the helpless, and enslaved
But to them all his efforts gave.
A man whose efforts knew no length
A Sampson, a towering pillar of strength
One with whom the world has dealt,
A humanitarian was Roosevelt.

Unselfishly, he did his job
To quiet Europe's war-torn mob,
Always striving, hoping, praying
For the peace with lives we're paying.
Looking forward to a bright day
When freedom's light would cast its ray,
And all the world would again be free,
Just as we've always dreamed would be.

Rest quietly, friend, your work is done.
But ours is only half begun,
We'll do our best to carry on,
Trying harder now that you are gone.

The chief is dead, yet lives the chief!
So we are compensated in our grief,
For he has left a wondrous plan
To be completed by God and man.

Rem-men-nis-sen at the U.S.O
By Burrell B. DeHaven
(a member of the Prometheans)
5/7/1943

I'm just rem-men-nis-sen a kinda slow ole sort a way;
Ain't thinken much about anything, ain't car'n much
About the day.

Kinda lazy, feeling kinda low.
Don't care much about anyone I know.
People 'round me dancing, some others, I think,
Romancing.

Soldiers play'n cards, soldiers play'n hard;
Young ladies pass and smile trying to make the
Time worthwhile.

Wonder if I know what I'm Miss'n?
Well I don't care 'cause I'm Rem-men-nis-sen.

LIST OF HOWARD UNIVERSITY SERVICE MEN AND WOMEN WHO SERVED IN WORLD WAR II

COMPLIED BY DORORHY PORTER WESLEY

The following pages display the military service information for the brave men and women of Howard University who served their country during World War II.

Abbreviations used:

1st LT	First Lieutenant	MAJ	Major
1st MUS	First Musician	MUS	Musician
2nd LT	Second Lieutennt	PFC	Private, First Class
AST	Assistant	PVT	Private
AVN CADET	Aviation Cadet	SA	Seaman Apprentice
BAND LDR	Band Leader	SGT	Sergeant
CPL	Corporal	SSC	Sergeant, Second Class
CPT	Captain	SSG	Staff Sergeant
E	Enlisted member	ST ASST	Staff Assistant
ENS	Ensign	TCPL	Technical Corporal
FLTO	Flight Officer	TEC	Technician
LT	Lieutenant	VOC	Voluntary Officer
LT COL	Lieutenant Colonel		Candidate
M SGT	Master Sergeant	W	Warrant Officer

Last Name	First Name	Rank	Service	
Addison	Richard	PVT	Co. B, 67th Infantry Training Battalion	
Alfred	Earle A.	1st LT	372nd Infantry, Co. F	
Allen	Fred	LT		
Allen	Fred L.	LT	795th Tank Destroyer Bat.	
Allen	George W.			
Anderson	Albert Victor			
Austin	Ralph E.	Chaplain	USA Replacement Service	
Avant	Edward R.			
Bailey	Joseph L.			
Banks	William	LT		
Banks, Jr.	William A.			
Barbee	Norvell D.	2nd LT	372nd Infantry	
Barker	Melvin A.	1st LT	372nd Infantry	
Barker	Wiley	PVT	300 TSS Flight	
Bates	Arthur V.			
Baynard	John P.	LT		
Beach	Phillip Alphonso			
Bell Jr.	Herman M.	LT		
Benton	Alexander	LT		
Berry	Alonzo	CPT	327th Infantry	
Berry	Earl	PVT		
Binford	Robert	E		

P.O.	Class	Degree	Affliation	HU College Affiliation
Camp Wolters, TX				
124 East 23rd Street	1937	MA		
		AB		
Fort Custer, MI	1937	MA		
		LLB		School of Law
	1932	MD, MED		
Fort McClelland, AL	1935			School of Religion / Divinity School
	1935	LLB		School of Law
	1937	LLB		School of Law
Camp Atterbury, IN				
		LLB		School of Law
31 West 110th Street, New York, NY	1942; 1947; 1955	BS; DDS		
31 West 110th Street, New York, NY		BA		
Jefferson Barracks, MO				
Fort Huachuca, AZ	1940	LLB		School of Law
	1938	BS, Cvl Eng.		
	1934	MD		
		LLB		School of Law
Fort Huachuca, AZ			Phi Beta Sigma	
Fort Dix, NJ	1931; 1935	BA; MED; MD		Medicine
Mithcell Field				
	1944			

Last Name	First Name	Rank	Service	
Bingham	Leroy E.	1st LT	Dental Corps	
Birch	Joseph N.	PVT	Co. I, 9th Quartermaster Regiment	
Birch	LaVerne B.		Ameican Red Cross	
Bivens	Courtland	E		
Blache	Julian O.	CPT	Station Hospital	
Black	Fred	LT		
Black	Gorham	LT		
Bolden	Edgar Lewis	LT	Walterboro Army Air Field	
Botts	Joseph			
Bradley	David Vernard	LT		
Bray	David E.	1st LT	372nd Infantry	
Brazington	Andrew	E		
Brice	John J.	W	Replacement Center	
Broadnax	Clarence H.	TCPL	First S.T.R., 23rd Co.	
Brooks	Charles W.	1st LT	Med. Corps, 703rd Med. San. Co.	
Brooks	William	LT	25th Infantry	
Brown	Daniel Nye	Chaplain	99th Fighter Squadron TAFS Tuskegee Ald.	
Brown	James Russell	Chaplain	Naval Reserve	
Brown	Leroy	PVT	Tuskegee Aviation Flying School	
Brown	Lorenzo Q.	LT, Chaplain	374th Engineer Battalion	
Brown	Mark		Recruit Receiving Center, Co. G.	

P.O.	CLASS	DEGREE	AFFLIATION	HU COLLEGE AFFILIATION
Fort Huachuca, AZ	1927	DDS		
Camp Lee, VA	1931	LW; LLB		
England				
	1944			
Fort Huachuca, AZ	1932	MD		
	1942			
	1942			
SC	1948	Elect. Eng.		
	Sr 1942			School of Music
	1936	MD; MED		
31 West 110th Street, New York, NY				
	1943			
Fort Bragg, NC				
Fort Benning, GA				
Fort Custer, MI				
Fort Huachuca, AZ		MS		
Tuskegee, AL				
Great Lakes, IL	1935	BD		
Tuskegee, AL	1928	LA, AB		
Camp Hood, TX; Fort Benning, GA	1940	MA		School of Religion/ Divinity School
Fort Meade, MD	1949	BA		

Last Name	First Name	Rank	Service	
Brown	Richard T.S.	1st LT	Army Chaplain Corps	
Brown	Robert A.	LT	Antitank Co., 25th Infantry	
Browne	Emerson			
Browne Jr.	Lester		Co. B, 9th ETB ERTC	
Bryant	William	2nd LT	U.S. Army, Educational Department of the Special Services Division	
Buckner	George W.	LT		
Bush	Charles V.		U.S. Air Force Academy	
Butcher	George W.	LT		
Butcher	James W.	2nd LT	Recreation Center	
Butler	DeRuyter A.	MAJ	372nd Infantry	
Butler	John W.	1st LT	Station Hospital D.C. 1	
Butler	Peter N.	TEC-5 (CPL)	666th Port Company	
Campbell	Ulysses	LT		
Carnegie	Wilbur L.	2nd LT	Col. C, 368th Infantry	
Carr	William	LT		
Carrington	M.T.	AS	Co. 1754 26th Battalion, U.S.N.T.S.	
Carter	Robert			
Carter	Robert L.			
Cash	Eugene	E		

P.O.	CLASS	DEGREE	AFFILIATION	HU COLLEGE AFFILIATION
Camp John T. Knight Transportation Corps Installation	1934			
Fort Huachuca, AZ				
Fort Devens, MA	1927	LLB		School of Law
Fort Belvoir, VA		LLB		School of Law
War Department, Washington, D.C.	1928; 1932; 1936	PC; AB; LLB		
	1942	DDS		College of Dentistry
CO Springs, CO		School of Engineering and Architecture	Alpha Phi Alpha	
	1941	DDS		College of Dentistry
Fort Huachuca, AZ				
31 West 110th Street, New York, NY	1928	MD		
Fort Huachuca, AZ				
Los Angeles Port of Embarkation				
	1939	DDS		College of Dentistry
Fort Huachuca, AZ				
	1940			
Camp Smalls, Great Lakes, IL	1948	MSW		
	1935			Medicine
	1940	LLB		School of Law
	1941	AB		

Last Name	First Name	Rank	Service	
Cato	Minto	ST ASST	American Red Cross, European Theater of Operations	
Cesne	Archibald D.	PVT		
Chandler	Jesse	CPT	318th Medical Battalion	
Chapman	Joseph H.	CPL	Transportation Corps	
Chase	Hyman Y.	MAJ	366th Infantry	
Clanagan	Frederick	SGT	95th Engineers General Service Regiment	
Cleland	William Alexander	LT	25th Station Hospital	
Cochran	Chappelle Cecil	LT		
Coggs	Theodore	E		
Colbert	Frank Lucius		U.S. Naval Training Station	
Coleburn	Nathaniel	E		
Collier	Vivian V.	ST ASST	American Red Cross	
Collins	Charles W.		U.S. Army Signal Corps	
Conquest	George	CPL	Officer Candidate Class #58	
Cook	Hugh	CPL	Co. E. 9th Regiment Quartermaster Replacement Training Center	
Cooper	Harry E.	PVT	84th Aviation Squadron	
Coppock	John W.	CPL	Company B. 446, Signal Construction Battalion	
Corbeirre	Tolem M.	1st LT	318th Medical Battalion	
Corprew	Theodore	1st LT	Advanced Pool, Medical Field Service School	

P.O.	CLASS	DEGREE	AFFLIATION	HU COLLEGE AFFILIATION
Camp Meade, MD				
Fort Huachuca, AZ	1934	BS		
European Theater of Operations				
Fort Devens, MA	1926; 1930	BS; MS		Medicine
PO 998, Seattle, WA	1950	BS		
Fort Jackson, SC		MD		
Fort Huachuca, AZ	1938; 1940	BS; MS		Medicine
	1940	AB		
Ninth Naval District, Great Lakes, IL		BS Zoology, Pharmacy		
	1944			
Fort Stills, OK				
Camp Lee, VA	1941	BS		
Jefferson Barracks, MO				
Langley Field, VA	Soph 1941			School of Music
Fort Huachuca, AZ				
Carlisle Barracks, Carlisle, PA				

Last Name	First Name	Rank	Service	
Dailey	Bertrand	CPL	Transportation Corps	
Darden	Gretie	1st LT	U.S. Army Nursing Service	
Dedmon	Jesse O.			
De Jarmon	La Marquis	SGT		
Dennis	John	PVT	Company F, 11th Quartermaster Regiment	
De Vermond	Kai		SS *Pan Royal*	
Dickerson	Herbert H.	SGT	339th Aviation Squadron	
Dickerson	Leonard	SGT		
Dishman	Clarence		U.S. Air Corps	
Dixon	Bernest	1st LT	372nd Infantry	
Dixon	Joseph W.	1st LT	795th T.D. Battalion	
Dowdell	Crawford B.	AVN CADET	99th Pursuit Squadron	
Dunguid	Herbert S.	LT		
Durden	Lewis Minyon	Chaplain		
Edelin	William B.	MAJ	Assistant Administrative Instructor, Tuskegee Army Air Field	
Edwards	Eric Paul	2nd LT	25th Infantry	
Eggleston	George L.	LT COL	372nd Infantry	

P.O.	CLASS	DEGREE	AFFLIATION	HU COLLEGE AFFILIATION
European Theater of Operations				
Fort Huachuca, AZ				Nurse, Freedmen's Hospital School of Nursing
Fort Devens, MA	1935	LLB		School of Law
Camp Lee, VA	1904	CER		
Port Master, NY				
Columbia Air Army Base, Columbia, SC	1945			School of Music
		Mechanical Engineering		
31 West 110th Street, New York, NY	1931	BA		
Fort Custer, MI	1941	BS		
Tuskegee, AL	1914	DDS		
	1942	DDS		College of Dentistry
Fort Dix, NJ	1942	MA		School of Religion/ Divinity School
Tuskegee, AL	1924; 1925	BA, MA		
Fort Huachuca, AZ	1941	BS		
31 West 110th Street, New York, NY	1923	AB		

Last Name	First Name	Rank	Service	
Elliot	Israel E.	1st LT	372nd Infantry	
English	Walter		99th Pursuit Squadron, Tuskegee Aviation Flying School	
Ewell	Costromer	1st LT	Station Hospital, D.C. 2	
Fairfax	James A.	CPL	Brookley Field	
Fellman	Sidney	LT		
Felton	Aliston			
Felton	Edgar	LT		
Felton	Edgar B.	CPT	92nd "Buffalo" Division; Fifth Army	
Ferrell	E. Lewis	PVT	Co. B, 3rd Platoon, 8th Battalion	
Fisher	J. Walters	LT		
Flagg	Charles	1st LT	366th Infantry	
Flagg	Leslie E.	LT	366th Infantry	
Florestano	Joseph M.	MUS		
Ford	Idella O.	2nd LT	U.S. Army Nursing Service	
Forman	Marquis	SGT		
Francis	Charles E.	2nd LT	Tuskegee Army Air Field	
Freeman	Edward	PVT	Company T, 6th Receiving Center	
Freeman	Susan E.	1st LT	U.S. Army Nursing Service	

P.O.	CLASS	DEGREE	AFFLIATION	HU COLLEGE AFFILIATION
31 West 110th Street New York, NY	1938	MD		
Tuskegee, AL	1932; 1934	AB, MA		
Fort Huachuca, AZ	1928	DDS		
Mobile, AL	1947	BA		
	1937	DDS		College of Dentistry
			Phi Beta Sigma	
Fort Benning, GA	1942		Phi Beta Sigma	
Northern Italy				
Fort Belvoir, VA	1941	LLB		School of Law
Fort Custis, MI				
Fort Devens, MA				
Fort Devens, MA				
134 Prince George Street, Annapolis, MD				
Fort Huachuca, AZ	1933			Freedmen's Hospital School of Nursing
Camp Lee, VA			Phi Beta Sigma	
Tuskegee, AL		BA, MA		
1222 Camp Upton, Upton, NY				
Fort Huachuca, AZ	1926			Freedmen's Hospital School of Nursing

Last Name	First Name	Rank	Service	
Friedenthal	Meyer	CPT	Medical Detachment; 34th A.H.	
Fuller	Samuel L.	1st LT	15th Air Force, Flying Mustangs	
Gaines	Thurston L.	Fighter Pilot	Tuskegee Army Airfield	
Gant	Duplain R.	SGT	Transportation Corps	
Gay	Randall Garfield	SA	Naval Reserves, Company 1623, U.S. Naval Training Station	
Gibson Jr.	Herschel P.	E	1902 Ordnance Company Ammunition	
Giles	William	1st SGT	792nd Ordnance Compnay; 92nd Infantry Division	
Goodull	P.E.	CPT		
Gordon	Alexander H.	SGT	93rd Division	
Gordon	Frank Carroll		U.S. Naval Training Station	
Gordon	Robert A.	Flight Instructor	Tuskegee Army Air Field	
Gould	Frederick	PVT		
Granger	Shelton		Charleston Port of Embarkation	
Grayson	Julian		M.P. Battalion	
Green	Elisabeth P.	ASST	American Red Cross	
Greene	Harry W.	1st LT	Station Hospital #3	
Greene	J.M.	CPT	366th Infantry	

P.O.	CLASS	DEGREE	AFFLIATION	HU COLLEGE AFFILIATION
Camp Cooke, CA				
Italy				
Tuskegee, AL	1943		Alpha Phi Alpha	
Los Angeles Port of Embarkation				
Great Lakes, IL				
MacDill Field, Tampa, Florida	1943			
Fort McClellan, AL	1944			
Fort Huachua, AZ				
Fort Huachuca, AZ	1935			School of Religion/ Divinity School
Great Lakes, IL				
	1939	BS	Alpha Phi Alpha	
Charleston, SC	1942	AB		
CA			Phi Beta Sigma	
Australia				
Fort Huachuca, AZ	1925	DDS		
Fort Devens, MA	1919	BS		

Last Name	First Name	Rank	Service	
Greene	Vernon F.	CPT	372nd Infantry	
Greens	Harry J.			
Griffin	James Clarke	Chaplain, CPT	10th Cavalry	
Grillo	Aveleo	E		
Hacker	C. Leroy	Chaplain	366th Division	
Hall	Charles R.	LT		
Hampey	Menvil	E		
Hardin	Herbert G.	LT	Co. A. 6th Battalion	
Harding	Leonard	E		
Harper	Emily May		American Red Cross; War Manpower Commission	
Harris	Middleton A.	ASST	American Red Cross	
Harris	Phillip A.W.	1st LT	Co. B, 8th Medical Trg. Battalion, Tuskeegee Army Air Field	
Harris	Robert E.	1st LT	Station Hospital, D.C. 2	
Harrison	Earl	1st LT	366th Infantry	
Hart	Bessie	2nd LT	U.S. Army Nursing Service	
Hawkins	Dorothea Mae		American Red Cross; European Theater of Operations	
Hayes	Ura T.	CPL	Headquarters Detachment, ASFTC; Army Service Forces Training Center	

P.O.	CLASS	DEGREE	AFFLIATION	HU COLLEGE AFFILIATION
31 West 110th Street, New York, NY				
Camp Lookitt, CA; Fort Riley, KS	1935			School of Religion/ Divinity School
	1943			
Fort Devens, MA	1937			School of Religion/ Divinity School
Fort Benning, GA	1940	LLB		School of Law
	1943			
Aberdeen Proving Grounds; Aberdeen, MD	1940	LLB		School of Law
	1944	CRAF		
	1931	AB		
Camp Lee, VA; Tuskegee, AL	1939	LLB		School of Law
Fort Huachuca, AZ				
Fort Devens, MA				
Fort Huachuca, AZ	1940			Freedmen's Hospital School of Nursing
Camp Lee, VA		MA	Phi Beta Sigma	

Last Name	First Name	Rank	Service	
Hendrick	Robert	LT		
Henry	Axel			
Hickman	Daniel	E		
Hinds	Leslie	1st LT	318th Medical Battalion	
Hines	G. Wilton	2nd LT	92nd Infantry Division	
Hines	Russell	M SGT	907th Air Base Security Battalion	
Hobson	H. Harrison	CPT		
Holliman	A.G.		U.S.N.T.S. Band	
Holmes	Jedekiah			
Holmes	Oliver W.	PVT	Provisional Battalion, Coast Anti-Aircraft Artillery	
Holsman	Hezikiah	1st MUS	U.S.N. Reserve Band	
Hopkins	John O.			
Hopkins	Thomas J.	CPT		
Howard	Weaver O.	CPT	372nd Infantry	
Howard III	Andrew J.	PVT	Bn. Hq. 774 M.T. Battalion	
Hungate	Thad L.	MAJ	Headquarters, Services of Supply, War Department	
Hunter	John G.	LT	366th Infantry	
Hunter	Charles Hatch	LT		
Hyman	Joshua	E		
Irving	Thomas E.	LT	25th Infantry	
Ivy	S. Laddie	VOC		

P.O.	CLASS	DEGREE	AFFLIATION	HU COLLEGE AFFILIATION
13½ Eagle Street, Asheville, NC	1940	MS		
		LLB		School of Law
	1944			
Fort Huachuca, AZ	1936	DDS		
Fort McClellan, AL	1934	BS, Civil Engineering		
Camp Rucker, AL	Soph 1939			School of Music
	1934	BS		
Hampton Institute, Hampton, VA	1938; 1947	BA, MASW		
			Phi Beta Sigma	
Camp Stewart, GA				
Hampton, VA				
	1936	LLB		School of Law
31 West 110th Street, New York, NY		MD		
March Field, Riverside, CA	1942	BS		
Pentagon Building, Washington, D.C.				Chairman, Board of Trustees
Fort Devens, MA				
Selfridge Field, MI	1939	MS		
Fort Huachuca, AZ				
Camp Eustis, VA	1940	LLB		School of Law

LAST NAME	FIRST NAME	RANK	SERVICE	
Jackson	Cleveland	SGT		
Jackson	Hugh	LT		
Jacobs	Clarence	LT	92nd Infantry Division	
James	Frederick Warfield	1st LT	Dental Corps, AUS	
Jarrett	George	PVT		
Jenkins	Pliny	LT	379th Engineer Battalion	
Johnson	Darneal F.	Chaplain		
Johnson	Jarone W.	1st LT	Station Hospital, Sec. 1, Medical Corps	
Johnson	Joshua	LT	Co. D, 277th Quartermaster Battalion	
Johnson	Julia Lilmarth	ST ASST	American Red Cross	
Johnson	Sarah	2nd LT	U.S. Army Nursing Service	
Johnson	Wilmot		O.C. S.	
Jones	Clarence	SGT	Headquarters Detachment; Chaplain Section 9th Quartermaster Regiment	
Jones	Elmer D.	2nd LT		
Jones	John Gassaway	PVT	318th Air Base Squadron, T.A.F.S.	
Jones	Perry	LT	124 E. 23rd Street New York, NY	
Jones	William P.	PVT	Co. D., 5th Battalion, 1st Training Regiment	
Jones Jr.	William P.	SGT	Co. D. 276th Quatermaster Battalion	

P.O.	Class	Degree	Affliation	HU College Affiliation
Camp Lee, VA	1930	MD		
	1942	AB		
Fort Huachuca, AZ	1937			
	1945			
Camp Shelby, MS	1940	BTH		
Fort Knox, KY	1932			School of Religion/ Divinity School
Fort Huachuca, AZ	1938	MD		
H.R.P.E. Newport News, VA				
	1940	AB		
Fort Huachuca, AZ	1941			Freedmen's Hospital School of Nursing
Fort Belvoir, VA			Phi Beta Sigma	
Camp Lee, VA	1941			School of Music
	1941	BS, Electrical Engineering		
Tuskegee, AL				
	1941	AB		
Fort McClellan, AL				
Camp Stoneman, Pittsburg, CA				

Last Name	First Name	Rank	Service	
Keene	William	PVT		
Kennedy	Ezekial			
Kerr	Oliver E.	2nd LT	Tuskegee Army Air Field	
Kotler	Solomon	LT		
Lake	William E.B.	LT	Recon Cavalry Troop, 93rd Infantry	
Lane	David P.	LT		
Lang	Zola Mae	1st LT	U.S. Army Nursing Service	
Larry	Milton Covington		American Red Cross	
Lawrence	George P.	CPT		
Lawson	Beatrix F.	LT		
Layton	Benjamin T.	2nd LT	369th Infantry, 93rd Division	
Lee	James	LT		
Leighton	George N.	1st LT	Officer's Mess	
Letcher	Henry M.	2nd LT	99th Pursuit Squadron	
Lewis	Clarence O.	LT		
Lewis	Colston A.			
Lightfoot	Jonartur	LT	318th Engineering Battalion, 93rd Division	
Lofton	Harry T.	LT COL	372nd Infantry	

P.O.	CLASS	DEGREE	AFFLIATION	HU COLLEGE AFFILIATION
Jefferson Barracks, St. Louis, MO			Phi Beta Sigma	
	Jr 1942			School of Music
Tuskegee, AL	1937			
	1937	DDS		College of Dentistry
Fort Huachuca, AZ				
	1942	DDS		College of Dentistry
Fort Huachuca, AZ	1940			Freedmen's Hospital School of Nursing
A.P.O. #887 New York, NY	1936	AB		
Fort Devens, MA	1939	LLB		School of Law
	1942	DDS		College of Dentistry
Fort Huachuca, AZ				
	1943			
Fort Huachuca, AZ	1940	AB		
Army Air Base, Tuskegee, AL	1933	BS	Phi Beta Sigma	Instructor, Ceramic Art, Awarded Bronze Medal
	1938	DDS		College of Dentistry
		LLB		School of Law
Fort Huachuca, AZ				
31 West 110th Street, New York, NY	1919	DIP		

Last Name	First Name	Rank	Service	
Lopez	George	E		
Lowery	Jessie	E		
Lucas	Wendell M.	1st LT	Mustang Fighter Group	
Lucas	Wendell M.	LT	25th Infantry	
Lundy	Rayfield	M SGT	1st Avenue Cantonment	
Mack	Aaron T.			
Madden	Osceola W.		U.S. Naval Training Station	
Madison	Robert	CPT		
Mangum	Arron	E		
Manly	John B.	CPT	Flight Surgeon, Medical Corps, U.S. Army Forces	
Manning	Walter F.	2nd LT	Tuskegee Army Air Field	
Manns	Mercer			
Martin	Graham	SSC	Ships Company, 18th Regiment	
Martin	Graham Edward	ENS	U.S. Naval Training Station	
Martin Jr.	J. Thomas	LT		
Matthews	Jerome E.	LT		
Matthews	Reginald S.			
Mayo	James A.	1st LT	372nd Infantry	
Mays	Charles	LT		

P.O.	Class	Degree	Affliation	HU College Affiliation
	1943			
Tuskegee, AL	1940	BS MS	ROTC, Howard University	
Fort Huachuca, AZ				Medicine
1st Avenue and Spokane, Seattle WA		LLB		School of Law
	1940	LLB		School of Law
Ninth Naval District, Great Lakes, IL		BA		
	1923	BS, Electrical (civil) Engineering		
	1943			
African Theater of Operations	1935	MD	Alpha Phi Alpha	Instructor of Surgery
Tuskegee, AL				
Camp Gordon, Augusta, GA				
Camp Robert Smalls, Great Lakes, IL				
Great Lakes, IL				
		LLB		School of Law
	1942	DDS		College of Dentistry
	1942	LLB		School of Law
31 West 110th Street, New York, NY	1953	MS		
Fort Huachuca, AZ			Phi Beta Sigma	

Last Name	First Name	Rank	Service	
McConnell	Wendell L.	LT	25th Infantry	
McCormick	Joseph P.	CPL	Headquarters Company, First Battalion, 370th Infantry	
McDonald	George	LT COL	Chief of Medical Services; Tuskegee Army Air Field	
McDowell	Thaddeus	PVT		
McGhee	Robert	PVT		
McGill	Theodora E.	ASST	American Red Cross	
McIver	James Emmett	SGT	Company B, 11th Quartermaster Training Regiment	
McKnight	Scott S.	CPT		
McLeod	Clarence E.	E		
Melton	William R.	LT	Tuskegee Army Air Field	
Miller	Theodore S.	2nd LT	Tuskegee Army Air Field	
Millin	Raphael O.	CPL	Co. A, 264th Quartermaster Battalion	
Minis	Frederick		Flying Squadron	
Miree	James			
Mitchell	Doyle	LT		
Moman Jr.	Robert M.	2nd LT	Infantry, 2nd Casual Co. 3rd Student Training Regiment	
Monroe	Oswald	1st LT	368th Infantry	
Moore	Archie L.	2nd LT	372nd Infantry	

P.O.	CLASS	DEGREE	AFFLIATION	HU COLLEGE AFFILIATION
Fort Huachuca, AZ	1939	LLB		School of Law
Camp Beckinridge, KY				
Tuskegee, AL		MD		
		Law		
Camp Lee, VA	1951			
	1933	DDS		College of Dentistry
	1941	LLB		School of Law
Tuskegee, AL				
Tuskegee, AL	1942		Omega Psi Phi	
Camp Kilmer, NJ	1940	LLB		School of Law
Tuskegee, AL			Phi Beta Sigma	
	1941	MD		
1900 H Street, N.E., Washington, D.C.				College of Medicine
Fort Benning, GA				
Fort Huachuca, AZ	1937	AB		
31 West 110th Street, New York, NY	1931; 1933	MA; GD; AM		

Last Name	First Name	Rank	Service	
Moore	Noah P.			
Moore	William	PVT	93rd Signal Squadron	
Moorhead	Clifford	E		
Moses	Edison	PVT		
Mosette	James	2nd LT	372nd Infantry	
Murphy	David J.	Aviation Candidate	Regimental Headquarters Service Company; 923rd Engineer Aviation Regiment; Tuskegee Army Air Field	
Murphy	Viola B.	ST ASST	American Red Cross	
Murphy Jr.	David J.		Army Aviation, Regt. H.W. and Service Co. 923rd Engineering	
Murray	Judson T.	CPL	Transportation Corps	
Nelson	John	E		
Nickens	H.	SGT	M.C.	
Nickens	James H.	LT	25th Station Hospital	
Orr	Herbert Roy	CPT	13th AAF Figther Command; died in service	
Parker	Albert F.	2nd LT		
Parker	Charles	E		
Parker	Mervin Orlando	LT	184th Field Artillery	
Parks	William	E		

P.O.	Class	Degree	Affliation	HU College Affiliation
Camp Stewart, GA		LLB	Phi Beta Sigma	School of Law
Fort Huachuca, AZ				
	1943			
31 West 110th Street, New York, NY				
Elgin Field, FL; Tuskegee, AL	1943			
				Payroll Bookeeper
Elgin Field, FL; Tuskegee, AL				
European Theater of Operations				
	1943			
Fort Bragg, NC			Phi Beta Sigma	
A.P.O. 601 New York, NY	1935; 1939	BS, MD		College of Medicine
South Pacific	1930; 1931; 1935	BS, Elect. Eng.; MS, Phys.	Kappa Alpha Psi	
	1943			
Fort Custer, MI	1936	BS		
	1942			

Last Name	First Name	Rank	Service	
Patton	Humphrey C.	FLT O	Tuskegee Army Air Field	
Penn	Hubert	PVT	Military Police Detachment (Quartermaster - cld.)	
Pettross	George E.P.	LT	Tuskegee Air Flight School	
Petty	Mary	1st LT	U.S. Army Nursing Service	
Phipps	Harold H.	LT	Dental Corps	
Piersawl	Harry H.	CPT	366th Infantry	
Pinckney	Theodore	CPT		
Pinkett Jr.	John R.		332nd Fighter Group; Headquarters, TAFS	
Pinn	J.R.	LT	Chaplain of Division Recently Landed	
Piper	Frederick	LT	25th Infantry	
Pogue	William F.	A.S.R.	U.S. Coast Guard	
Pollard	Robert L.	MAJ	366th Infantry	
Pope	Ernest	E		
Powell	John Benjamin	PVT	Engineering Corps; Headquarters Company 823rd Engineering Battalion	
Pratt	Charles A.			
Price	Albert	2nd LT	366th Infantry	
Quick	Odia F.			
Raiford	R. Douglass	LT		

P.O.	CLASS	DEGREE	AFFILIATION	HU COLLEGE AFFILIATION
Tuskegee, AL			Alpha Phi Alpha	
Fort Eustis, VA				
Tuskegee, AL	1935	AB		
Fort Huachuca, AZ	1940			Freedmen's Hospital School of Nursing
Fort Huachuca, AZ	1941	DDS		College of Dentistry
Fort Devens, MA	1934	AB		
Tuskegee, AL				
Liberia, Africa		DD		
Fort Huachuca, AZ				
Manhattan Beach Training Station, Brooklyn, NY	1945	MD		
Fort Devens, MA	1934	LLB		School of Law
	1943			
New York, NY	1941	BS, Engineering		
	1935	LLB		School of Law
Fort Devens, MA	1942	AB		
	1940	LLB		School of Law
	1942	AB		

Last Name	First Name	Rank	Service	
Raines	William C.		Willa Brown Aviation School	
Rampey	Melville E.		Co. C, 10th Engineer Training Battalion	
Randall	Constance M.	ASST	American Red Cross	
Randall	Phillip J.	LT	372nd Infantry	
Randall	Steward			
Randolph	Ethel	Medical Technician	Station Hospital	
Randolph	Lenard	1st LT	368th Infantry	
Randolph	Lester	E		
Randolph, Jr.	William A.	2nd LT	372nd Infantry	
Rapley	Lucia	2nd LT	U.S. Army Nursing Service	
Reddick	Vernon			
Reeves	William Godfrey	SSG	Battery C, 99th A.A.	
Reid	Daniel T.	LT	Corps of Engineers	
Reid	Duaa T.		Officers Training Corps	
Reid	William H.	1st LT	372nd Infantry	
Richardson	Milton	AVN CADET	99th Pursuit Squadron	
Richardson	Milton R.	LT	Tuskegee Army Air Field	
Ridley	Peter S.		American Red Cross	
Ridley Jr.	John H.	SGT	Air Corps	

P.O.	Class	Degree	Affliation	HU College Affiliation
Chicago, IL C.A.A.				
Engineer Replacement Training Center; Fort Belvoir, VA				
128 W. 138th Street, 5H, New York, NY	1937	BS		
	1940			Medicine
Fort Huachuca, AZ	1935	MS		
Fort Huachuca, AZ				
	1943			
31 West 110th Street, New York, NY				
Fort Huachuca, AZ	1934			Freedmen's Hospital School of Nursing
A.P.O. 869	1942			
EORP the ERTC, Fort Leonard Wood, MO				
Fort Belvoir, VA			Phi Beta Sigma	
Fort Dix, NJ				
Tuskegee, AL				
Tuskegee, AL	1939		Omega Psi Phi	
London, England	1931	MS		
Buckley Field, CO				

Last Name	First Name	Rank	Service	
Riggs	Henry L.	CPT	Tuskegee Army Air Field	
Riley	John			
Roberts	Lawrence F.	Aviation Candidate	Tuskegee Army Air Field	
Robinson	George Dewey	Chaplain		
Robinson	Norman	2nd LT	Company H, 366th Infantry	
Robinson	Sylvester			
Robinson	W.			
Robinson	Walter F.			
Royston	John E.			
Scott	Blanche L.	3rd Officer	Womens Army Auxillary Corps, Officers Quarters T507	
Scott	Gordan A.	SGT	480th Port Battalion	
Shaed	Gregory W.	1st LT	795th Tank Destroyer Bat.	
Sherman	Amelius	2nd LT	368th Infantry	
Sideboard	Henry Y.	Chaplain, CPT	371st Infantry Reginment	
Sims	Roger Bernard		U.S. Air Force Academy	
Skinner	John W.	1st LT	Station Hospital, D.C. 1	
Slade	Jessie	SGT	99th Pursuit Squadron	
Smith	Avery J.	Field Director	American Red Cross	
Smith	Benjamin			
Smith	Clarence	2nd LT	368th Infantry	

P.O.	CLASS	DEGREE	AFFILIATION	HU COLLEGE AFFILIATION
Tuskegee, AL	1940	MD	Alpha Phi Alpha	
	1944			School of Music
Tuskegee, AL	attended 1940 to 1942			
Camp Davis, NC	1941	BD		School of Religion/ Divinity School
Fort Devens, MA	1942	BS		
	1941	LLB		School of Law
		MD		
	1939	LLB		School of Law
	1940	LLB		School of Law
Army Post Branch, Fort Des Moines, Des Moines, IA				
U.S.A. Base, Norfolk, VA				
Fort Custer, MI	1934	MD		
Fort Huachuca, AZ				
Camp Robinson, AR	1938			School of Religion/ Divinity School
CO Springs, CO				
Fort Huachuca, AZ	1942	DDS		
Tuskegee, AL	1943			
	1939			School of Music
Fort Huachuca, AZ				

Last Name	First Name	Rank	Service	
Smith	Darwin	LT		
Smith	Emory	LT		
Smith	Jocelyn	LT		
Smith	Robert Anton	1st MUS	U.S. Naval Reserve Aviation Base	
Smith	Robert			
Smith	Theus	PFC	941st Guard Squadron.	
Smith Jr.	Alexander	2nd LT		
Smith Jr.	Arthur D.	BAND LDR		
Smith Jr.	Daniel H.	PVT	Army Replacement Center	
Snipes	George	PVT		
Snowden	O. Phillip	SGT	Company I, II Quartermasters Training Regiment	
Stamps	George			
Stanmore	L. Barnwell	1st LT	Headquarters 598 F.A. Battalion	
Starnes	Walter	SGT	Motor Pool Branch, 7 S.C.	
Stephenson	William W.	Pilot	Aviation Cadet Corps	
Stevens	Rutherford	1st LT	366th Infantry	
Stewart	Robert	CPT	795th Tank Destroyer Battalion	
Stewart	Willard C.	LT	Company K. 366th Infantry	
Strange	Wilfred E.	PVT	390th Engineer Regiment; Company Headquarters and Service	
Strickland	Wilbur	MAJ		

P.O.	Class	Degree	Affliation	HU College Affiliation
Camp Lee, VA				
1707 2nd Street, N.W., Washington, D.C.	1942	AB		
	1944			
Peru, IN	1942			
	1940			School of Music
T.A.F.S; Tuskegee, AL	1932	LLB		School of Law
Fort Eustis, VA	1950	DDS		
Fort Meade, MD	1939	BA		
Camp Lee, VA				
Indian Gap, PA			Phi Beta Sigma	
Camp Breckinridge, KY				School of Religion/ Divinity School
Camp Carson, CO	1929			
Tuskegee Army Airfield				
Fort Devens, MA	1939			Medicine
Fort Custer, MI				
Fort Devens, MA	1941	BA	Phi Beta Sigma	
Camp Claiborne, Alexandria, LA				
	1931	MD		

Last Name	First Name	Rank	Service	
Strother	Leonard	E		
Syphax	William C.	2nd LT	Tuskegee Army Airfield	
Talbot	Edgar	PVT		
Taylor	Carl B.	LT		
Taylor	Ordie	LT		
Taylor	Robert E.	SSG	Army Flying School, Medical Department	
Taylor Jr.	Halley B.	1st LT	Medical Corps; Tuskegee Army Air Field	
Taylor Jr.	Ordie P.	LT	92nd Cavalry Ren. Troop	
Teabuae	Ralph D.	MAJ	Station Hospital 3	
Teacheau	Ralph B.	MAJ		
Thalley	Bruce	LT		
Thomas	George	LT		
Thompson	Floyd F.	LT		
Thompson	Frank			
Thompson	Robert	E		
Thompson	Roland	PVT	432nd Engineers Co. D1	
Thurston	Roger			
Tinmey Jr.	William A.	PVT	733rd M.P. Battalion	
Turner	Andrew D.	CPT, LT	15th Air Force, Tuskegee Aviation Flying School	

P.O.	Class	Degree	Affliation	HU College Affiliation
	1943			
Tuskegee, AL		BS	Alpha Phi Alpha	
Camp Croft, SC				
Fort Washington, MD	1943		Phi Beta Sigma	
	1943			
Tuskegee, AL				
Tuskegee, AL	1938m 1942	BS, MD		
Fort McClellan, AL				
Fort Huachuca, AZ				
	1917	DDS		College of Dentistry
	1941	AB		
	1941	AB		College of Medicine
	1942	DDS		College of Dentistry
	1941			College of Medicine
	1942			
Camp Gordon, GA	1951	BME		School of Music
	1939			College of Medicine
Randolph Park, Tuscon, AZ	1937	LLB		School of Law
Italy; Tuskegee, AL				

Last Name	First Name	Rank	Service	
Turner	Anthony Harris	1st LT	795th Tank Destroyer Bat.	
Turner	Leonard F.	LT	Mediterranean Theatre of Operations, Tuskegee Army Air Field	
Tyson	James G.	Club Director	American Red Cross	
Valdes	Caesar	1st LT	Dental Officer, Tuskegee Army Air Field	
Valentine	Raymond J.			
Van Buren	George B.	LT	609th Ordnance Company; Athletic Officer	
Vickers	Carl R.	LT		
Wake	Wendell	LT		
Walker	Leroy	E		
Wall	N. Marie		Ameican Red Cross	
Wallace	John A.L.	1st LT	372nd Infantry	
Ward	Hampton H.	PFC	Headquarters Detachment 70th Ordnance Battalion (MM) Q	
Warner	Granville W.	1st LT	15th Air Force, Flying Mustangs	
Washington	L. Barnwell	Chaplain, 1st LT	371st Infantry; 598th Field Artillary Battalian	
Watson	S.P.	LT		
Watts	Frederick Payne	1st LT		
Weaver	Bruce T.			
Webb	Edward			
Weeks	Leroy	LT		

P.O.	CLASS	DEGREE	AFFILIATION	HU COLLEGE AFFILIATION
Fort Custer, MI	1935	BS		
			Kappa Alpha Psi	
	1929, 1932	AB, LLB	NAACP	
Tuskegee, AL	1935	DDS		
	1935	LLB		School of Law
	1941			
	1942	DDS		College of Dentistry
	1942	DDS		College of Dentistry
	1944			
London, England				
31 West 110th Street, New York, NY				
Fort Huachuca, AZ	1941, 1952	Certificate in Social Work; MSW		
Italy				
Camp Robinson, AR; Fort McClellan, AL				
Tuskegee				
515 North Arlington Avenue Baltimore, MD	1927	MA		
Fort Meade, MD		LLB		School of Law
	Sr 1937			School of Music
	1939			Medicine

Last Name	First Name	Rank	Service	
Wheatley	Luis Andres	PVT	17th Special Service Unit, 93rd Division	
Wheeler	Francis X.		3112 Park Place (home address)	
Wheeler	William M.	2nd LT	Tuskegee Army Air Field	
Whisonant	Lawrence	LT	93rd Division, 17th Special Service Unit	
White	Quincy	LT		
Whyte	James W.	LT	Tuskegee Army Air Field	
Wiley	J. Otis	SA	United States Naval Reserves, Co. 1622 28th Battalion, 18th Regiment	
Wilkins	Ralph D.	LT	Tuskegee Army Air Field	
Wilkinson, Jr.	F.D.	LT	372nd Infantry	
Williams	Bryant H.	SGT		
Williams	Robert	LT	366th Infantry	
Williams	Yancey	1st LT	Infantry Reserve Corps	
Willis	William		United States Coast Guard	
Wilson	Oliver W.	LT		
Wilson	Robert W.	CPT	ROTC, Howard University	
Wimms	Harry E.	PVT	Co. A. 5th Battalion	
Winder	Earl T.	CPT		
Winthrop	Charles R.	CPT	372nd Infantry	
Wood	Crozet	Dietitian	Station Hospital	
Wood	Ernestine		Womens Army Auxillary Corps	

P.O.	Class	Degree	Affliation	HU College Affiliation
Fort Huachuca, AZ	1939	B	Phi Beta Sigma	School of Music
	1950	DDS		Medical School
Tuskegee, AL				
Fort Huachuca, AZ	1941	B. Music	Phi Beta Sigma	School of Music
Tuskcgcc, AL			Alpha Phi Alpha	
Camp Robert Smalls, U.S.N.T.S. Great Lakes, IL				
Tuskegee, AL	1943			
285 Powell Street, Brooklyn, NY	1942	AB		
	1923	DIP		
Fort Devens, MA	1940	BS, Architecture		
	1941			
Manhattan Beach Training Station, Brooklyn, NY	1942	AB		
Camp Livingston, LA				
Washington, D.C.				
Fort McClellan, AL				
	1927	BS, Architecture		
31 West 110th Street, New York, NY		BA		
Camp Livingstone, LA				

Last Name	First Name	Rank	Service	
Woodford	Hackley	1st LT	Medical Corps, 703rd San. Med. Co.; Medical Corps; Tuskegee Army Air Field	
Woods, Jr	Arthur D.			
Wormley	Lowell			
Wyatt	William	PVT	Headquarters Battery 598 F.A.B.N.	

P.O.	CLASS	DEGREE	AFFLIATION	HU COLLEGE AFFILIATION
Fort Custer, MI; Tuskegee, AL	1940	MD	Alpha Phi Alpha	
	1931	MD		
Camp Breckenridge, KY				

NOTES

Introduction

1. Benjamin Quarles, *The Negro in the American Revolution* (Chapel Hill: University of North Carolina Press, 1996).

2. James M. McPherson, *The Negro's Civil War: How American Negroes Felt and Acted During the War for the Union* (New York: Vintage Books: Random House, 1965), 164.

3. Ibid.

4. Ibid.

5. Benjamin Quarles, *The Negro and the Civil War* (New York: Plenum Publishing, 1953), 24–39.

6. Ibid.

7. "The Trial of a Negro" *(NY) Tribune,* June 9, 1944; General Correspondence, 1944–1945: 291.2 0–Negroes, Adjutant General Section, Administration Branch, General Correspondence, Headquarters, European Theater of Operations, U.S. Army (World War II), Record Group 498, National Archives at College Park, College Park, Maryland.

8. "Let's Look at Rape," General Correspondence, 1944–1945: 291.2 0–Negroes, Adjutant General Section, Administration Branch, General Correspondence, Headquarters, European Theater of Operations, U.S. Army (World War II), Record Group 498, National Archives at College Park, College Park, Maryland.

Chapter 1

9. George E. Hall, "Howard and the War," *Howard University Journal* 14 no. 21 (March 30, 1917): 1, 7.

10. Ibid, 7.

11. "Howard Loyalty," *Howard University Journal* 14 no. 21 (March 30, 1917): 5.

12. Rayford Logan, *Howard University: The First One Hundred Years* (New York: New York University Press, 1967), 183; "Howard University in the Great War," *Howard University Catalog* (1918): 46.

13. Walter Dyson, *Howard University: The Capstone of Negro Education, A History: 1867–1940* (Washington, D.C.: Howard University Graduate School, 1941), 70–71.

14. "Howard University in the Great War," 38.

15. Dyson, *Howard University*, 74; *Howard University Catalog*, 1920; "Howard Spirit at Fort Des Moines," *Howard University Journal* 15, no. 1 (October 12, 1917): 1; "Howard University in the Great War," 39.

16. Dyson, *Howard University*, 70.

17. Elsie H. Brown, "The Red Cross Unit at Howard University" *Howard University Journal* 14 no. 21 (March 30, 1917): 2, 3.

18. Ibid.

19. Dyson, *Howard University*, 72; "Howard University in the Great War," 43.

20. "Howard University and National Defense," *Howard University Bulletin* (April 1942): 18, 104, 163, 248.

21. Ibid., 19.

22. Ibid., 18.

23. Ibid., 18.

24. Ibid.

25. Ibid., 21.

26. Ibid.

27. Ibid., 19.

28. "Howard University in World Wars One and Two," *Howard University Catalog* (Washington, D.C: Howard University, 1945), 55.

29. *Howard University Bulletin* (April 1941): 3.

30. Ibid., 4.

31. *Howard University Bulletin* (April 1941): 7, 21.

32. *Howard University Bulletin* (April 1942): 3.

33. "Howard University Honors 65 Student Enlisted Reserves Who Left for Armed Forces," *Howard University Bulletin* (April 1943): 16.

34. "Howard University in World Wars One and Two," 53.

35. Ibid.

36. Ibid., 54.

37. See Appendix D.

38. "Seventy Sixth Commencement—Fall Convocation," *Howard University Bulletin* (February 1945): 4–5.

39. "Howard Opens Office for Veterans of World War 2," *Howard University Bulletin* (February 1945): 15.

40. "Veterans Counseling and Advisory Service," *Howard University Catalog* (1945–46): 65–66.

41. "The Education of Veterans," *Howard University Bulletin* (October 1947): 44.

42. *Bison*, 1947.

43. Constitution of the Prometheans.

44. Origins of the Prometheans, Constitution of the Prometheans.

45. Origins of the Prometheans.

46. Merze Tate to Mordecai Johnson, Folder 19, Prometheans Collection, Manuscript Division, Moorland Spingarn Research Center, Howard University [hereafter MSRC].

47. Prometheans Newsletter, January 1945. Folder 19, Prometheans Collection, MSRC.

48. Prometheans Newsletter, January 1946. Folder 19, Prometheans Collection, MSRC.

49. Byron Turnquest to Merze Tate, Folder 19, Prometheans Collection, MSRC.

50. Sarah Khan, "World War II Black Veterans Group Disbands, But Friendships Remain." *Washington Post*, August 13, 2011, https://www.washingtonpost.com/local/world-war-ii-black-veterans-group-disbands-but-friendships-remain/2011/08/13/gIQAAac2DJ_story.html?utm_term=.a9e61280b281.

51. Gerri Majors, "Society World," *Jet* 41, no. 12 (December 16, 1971).

52. "World War II Prometheans Hold Reunion in Chicago," *Jet* 46, no. 24 (September 5, 1974).

53. Khan, "World War II Black Veterans," 1.

54. "Vietnam Week Closes with Peace Mobilization Tomorrow!!" *Hilltop* 49, no. 2 (April 14, 1967): 1; "Confrontation!!" *Hilltop* 49, no. 3 (April 28, 1967): 5.

Chapter 2

55. "The Military Department," *Howard University Catalog* (1869–70): 71.

56. Ibid.

57. Ibid.; Logan, *Howard University*, 53.

58. Dyson, *Howard University*, 53.

59. Ibid.

60. Ibid.

61. Ibid.

62. Logan, *Howard University*, 54.

63. Logan, *Howard University*, 180; Dyson, *Howard University*, 72.

64. Student Army Training Camp, Statement of Purpose, Folder 25, Thomas Montgomery Gregory Collection, MSRC.

65. Ibid.

66. Logan, *Howard University*, 180; Dyson, *Howard University*, 72.; Assignment of Officers at Howard University, Folder 24, Thomas Montgomery Gregory Collection, MSRC.

67. Logan, *Howard University*, 180. "Howard in the Great War," 42.

68. "World War II Prometheans Hold Reunion in Chicago"; Khan, "World War II Black Veterans."

69. "The ASTRP at Howard," *Howard University Bulletin* (November 1944): 21.

70. Logan, *Howard University*, 352.

71. Ibid., 353–54.

72. Ibid.; "Howard in the Great War."

73. *Bison*, 1923; Logan, *Howard University*, 183.

74. *Bison*, 1923.

75. Logan, *Howard University*, 195, 207.

76. *Howard University Catalog* (1919–20): 180–81.

77. Logan, *Howard University*, 435.

78. *Bison*, 1923; Logan, *Howard University*, 435.

79. Logan, *Howard University*, 217

80. Ibid., 220–21.

81. Ibid.

82. Ibid., 277–78.

83. *Bison*, 1928.

84. Ibid., 1932.

85. Logan, *Howard University*, 435.

86. *Bison*, 1967.

87. Logan, *Howard University*, 409.

88. "ROTC Unit Rated Best in US," *Howard University Bulletin* (December 1948): 16.

89. *Bison*, 1949, 1951.

90. *Bison*, 1951.

91. Ibid., 1968.

92. Ibid., 1966.

93. Ibid., 1969.

94. "Hilltop Poll: Students Say No to Nabrit, ROTC," *Hilltop* 50, no. 7 (October 27, 1967): 2; "Men Students Express Varied Views on ROTC," *Hilltop* vol. 50, no. 4 (October 13, 1967): 2.

95. Toni Ellis, "Nabrit, Snowden, Hershey Hanged Hearings Protested," *Hilltop* 49, no. 23 (April 21, 1967): 1.

96. "Student Favors ROTC Program," *Hilltop* 49, no. 2 (April 21, 1967): 2.

97. "ROTC Policy Voted On," *Hilltop* 49, no. 3 (April 28, 1967): 6.

98. Brenda Adams and Bobby Isaac, "Over 150 Walkout on Nabrit," *Hilltop* 50, no. 2 (September 22, 1967): 1; John Turner, "ROTC Issues Still Unresolved," *Hilltop* 50, no. 3 (October 5, 1967): 2.

99. "Freshman Walk Out to Protest ROTC," *Hilltop* 50, no. 4 (October 13, 1967): 1.

100. *Bison*, 1968.

101. Ibid., 1970.

102. Ibid.

Chapter 3

103. Marshall, George, Folder 100, Howard University Men and Women in the Armed Forces Collection [hereafter AFC], MSRC.

104. Scott, Anastasia, Folder 137, AFC, MSRC.

105. Ibid.

106. Sideboard, Henry, Folder 141, AFC, MSRC.

107. Ibid.

108. Ibid.

109. Marshall, John, Folder 101, AFC, MSRC.

110. Williams, Eva Mae, Folder 160, AFC, MSRC.

111. Holmes, Geneva, Folder 69, AFC, MSRC.

112. Williams, Rollin, Folder 161, AFC, MSRC.

113. Johnson, Darneal, Folder 77, AFC, MSRC.

114. Sideboard, Henry, Folder 141, AFC, MSRC.

115. Leighton, George, Folder 86, AFC, MSRC.

116. Ibid

117. Lovell, John, Folder 90, AFC, MSRC.

118. McDaniel, Robert, Folder 108, AFC, MSRC

119. Leighton, George, Folder 86, AFC, MSRC

120. Marshall, George, Folder 100, AFC, MSRC

121. Lundy, Folder 94, AFC, MSRC

122. Pley, Lucia, Folder 126, AFC, MSRC

123. McBeth, Harry C., Folder 104, AFC, MSRC.

124. Clanagan, Frederic, Folder 27, AFC, MSRC.

125. Clanagan, Frederic, Folder 27, AFC, MSRC.

126. Davis, Edgar, Folder 34, AFC, MSRC.

127. Lovell, John, Folder 90, AFC, MSRC.

128. Williams, Rollin C., Folder 161, AFC, MSRC.

129. Raynor, J.E., Folder 128, AFC, MSRC.

130. Keaton, James H., Folder 83, AFC, MSRC.

131. Robinson, John C., Folder 135, AFC, MSRC.

132. Snipes, George, Folder 142, AFC, MSRC.

133. Walker, George, Folder 151, AFC, MSRC.

134. Clanagan, Frederic, Folder 27, AFC, MSRC.

135. Fisk, Marvin, Folder 48, AFC, MSRC.

136. Luck, Thomas, Folder 93, AFC, MSRC.

137. Hobbs, Thaddeus, Folder 67, AFC, MSRC.

138. Luck, Thomas, Folder 93, AFC, MSRC.

139. Lucas, Wendell M., Folder 92, AFC, MSRC.

140. Powell, John, Folder 120, AFC, MSRC; Quick, John D., Folder 124, AFC, MSRC.

141. Jerry, Folder 165, AFC, MSRC.

INDEX

ABOUT THE AUTHOR

Lopez D. Matthews Jr. is the manager of the Digital Production Center and digital production librarian for the Howard University Libraries and the Moorland Spingarn Research Center. He is also the history subject specialist for the library. He teaches courses in African American, United States and world history at Coppin State University. Matthews received a BA in history from Coppin State University in 2004, a master's degree in public history and archival administration in 2006 and a doctorate in U.S. history from Howard University in 2009. Currently, he is a commissioner on the Maryland Commission on African American History and Culture, advisory board of the Banneker-Douglass Museum in Annapolis and a member of the board of directors of the Reginald F. Lewis Museum of Maryland African American History and Culture in Baltimore. He has published several articles and is the editor of several volumes, including *Liberating Minds…Liberating Society: Black Women in the Development of American Culture and Society* and *The History of Alpha Phi Alpha: Origins of the Eastern Region.*

Visit us at
www.historypress.net

CPSIA information can be obtained
at www.ICGtesting.com
Printed in the USA
LVHW081558300119
605806LV00010B/219/P

Mann Act which makes it illegal to transport women across state lines for "illicit purposes." His actual crime? He had white girlfriends. For fifteen years, left-wing filmmaker Ken Burns and actor Sylvester Stallone tried to get Johnson pardoned. Presidents George W. Bush and Barack Obama both refused.

Trump commuted the sentence of Alice Johnson, who was convicted of and given a longer sentence for a serious but nonviolent drug offense.

Trump secured the southern border. Most illegal aliens entering from our southern border are unskilled, lacking even a high school education. This means they compete against unskilled black and brown Americans for jobs while putting downward pressure on their wages. Peter Kirsanow, a commissioner of the US Civil Rights Commission, in his written testimony before the Senate Subcommittee on Immigration said that "not only do illegal immigrants compete for jobs with African-Americans, but that competition drives down wages for the jobs that are available."

Professor George Borjas of Harvard University has written: "Illegal immigration reduces the wages of native workers by an estimated $99 to $118 billion a year...A theory-based framework predicts that the immigrants who entered the country from 1990 to 2010 reduced the average annual earnings of American workers by $1,396 in the short run. Because immigration (legal and illegal) increased the supply of workers unevenly, the impact varies across skill groups, with high school dropouts being the most negatively affected group."[68]

---

68   "Borjas: Immigration and the American Worker,"
       NumbersUSA, October 13, 2015, https://www.numbersusa.
       com/resource-article/immigration-and-american-worker.

And Trump supported school choice. In 2017, *Politico* reported that the Trump administration quietly reversed an Obama-era policy of denying vouchers to low-income DC students who already attend private schools.[69] "We can now provide awards to those students, going into effect next school year," said Rachel Sotsky, executive director of Serving Our Children, a nonprofit that administers DC's Opportunity Scholarship Program—the nation's only federally funded voucher program.

These are all areas in which I, and the Republican party at large, remain grateful to Trump. Still, given the other rising stars in the Republican Party, I will be surprised if everyone rallies around Trump in the primaries. I'm flattered, though, that the likes of Alec Baldwin sees so much of him in me. "Larry Elder is a dangerous idiot—I mean Trump-level dangerous," Baldwin said when I ran against Newsom. (Baldwin's statement hasn't aged well....)

As for the Democrats gunning for the nomination in 2024, I have not been so impressed. Consider Pete Buttigieg. Here's a guy with minimal experience and one of the most glib attitudes I've seen in my life. He's just like Obama—only white. He wants to spend, tax, and regulate. He claims again and again that racism is a major problem in America. For him, even highways are racist.

I've already addressed Newsom's shortcomings, but not yet Kamala Harris, another California export who would

---

69   Caitlin Emma, "Trump Administration Reverses Obama Policy on D.C. Vouchers," *POLITICO*, May 5, 2017, https://www.politico.com/tipsheets/morning-education/2017/05/trump-administration-reverses-obama-policy-on-dc-vouchers.

instantly be the Democratic nominee if Biden were forced off the ticket. Republicans may scoff and mock Harris, but make no mistake, she is dangerous. She's a valuable asset in Southern states. Blacks are half of the Democratic voters and a majority of those are black females. They love Kamala Harris, and they feel she's being picked on. There's no reason to feel that she won't be a credible candidate if she ran for president. She had a disastrous presidential campaign in 2020, but she's not a fool. We underestimate her at our peril.

Of course, Biden will likely be the nominee, no matter what other Democrats may toss their hat in the ring. But, let's take a brief tour of the country under his rule.

Joe Biden is increasingly unpopular, defined by runaway inflation, high gas prices, surging crime, and the out-of-control southern border. President Biden's approval rating—hovering around thirty-nine percent after the midterm elections—is the lowest in history for any president at this point in his presidency since poll tracking began in 1945.[70]

Meanwhile, elections in San Francisco, New York, and Virginia show voters rejecting Democrats' failed policies nationwide. Voters in San Francisco recalled three, hyper-left-wing school board members. Voters in San Francisco County, by over 60 percent, recalled their soft-on-crime district attorney. Joe Biden's own pollster described the circumstances as "the worst political climate" of his lifetime. Republicans won back the House during the 2022 midterm elections, while the

---

70   Lange, Jason "Biden approval ticks lower as Democrats brace for midterm losses-Reuters/Ipsos" Reuters, November 8, 2022. https://www.reuters.com/world/us/biden-approval-ticks-lower-democrats-brace-midterm-losses-reutersipsos-2022-11-07/

Senate remains narrowly divided. This puts Republicans in a position to rein in Biden's spending. But that's not enough. They have a responsibility to use their power for good.

We need to decide what kind of nation we are. As President Biden said, "This isn't about being bogged down in the past. This is about making sure the past isn't buried...That's what great nations do. They don't bury the truth, they face up to it." So what is the Republican plan to rein in spending, given that most of the spending is on automatic pilot, and the size and intrusiveness of government?

Medicare/Medicaid/Obamacare take the biggest chunk, and, combined with Social Security, these programs (aka "entitlements") take more than half of government (aka "taxpayer") dollars. Next is income security, which includes: general retirement and disability insurance; federal employee retirement, disability and military retirement; unemployment compensation; housing assistance; nutrition assistance; foster care; Supplemental Security Income; and the earned income and child tax credits. They are followed, in decreasing order, by national security and interest on the debt. Combined, these programs consume almost all federal spending.

When then president Barack Obama signed the Affordable Care Act into law, Republicans called it costly, intrusive, and a giant leap toward the Democrats' ultimate goal: single-payer healthcare. Republicans vowed to repeal it. Candidate Donald Trump promised "to replace Obamacare with something better." But Obamacare became increasingly popular, and Republicans failed to offer a "replacement." Republicans stopped calling for its repeal.

appears to be our only hope to stop the spending rampage. Few Republicans are calling for this. Their silence is deafening.

I addressed these issues, as well as so many others when I ran in the recall election. I didn't win that one, but without my candidacy, I believe many more people's eyes would have remained closed to the truth about their state. As I look at the country, I am optimistic. More than three decades on the air and in television have shown me that people are open to the truth when someone presents it with conviction.

We have a country to save.

When Ronald Reagan first ran for California governor in 1966, his opponents were quick to point out that he said Social Security should be "voluntary." But he soon dropped the idea and never again suggested it. As a presidential candidate in 1980, Reagan promised to abolish the new Department of Education. By the time he left office eight years later, the department had not only survived but was bigger than when he entered office.

Former president George W. Bush promoted a plan to allow workers to direct a portion of their Social Security contribution into a private savings account that could be used to invest in the stock market. Democrats pounced, calling the "privatization" plan risky and dangerous. Pelosi later called Bush's increasingly unpopular idea a "political gift" for Democrats. Republicans, who once supported the idea, ran away from it, and Bush dropped it.

Both parties spend. But campaigning to reduce, let alone take away programs, is political suicide. And there is increasingly less discussion or even concern about the growing national debt. The only path forward is to tie the the hands of Congress through an amendment to the US Constitution that fixes government spending to a set percentage of our gross domestic product, with exceptions for war or natural disasters.

Under the Constitution, Article V allows states the power to call a Convention of States to propose amendments. Thirty-four states must agree to do so. Over the past few years, nineteen state legislatures have already endorsed the idea. That's more than halfway there. Another fifteen have legislation pending. Once considered a pie-in-the-sky fantasy, it now